# THE TROUBLED GENERATION

# THE TROUBLED

# GENERATION

## Toward Understanding and Helping

## The Young Adult

By RUDOLPH M. WITTENBERG

ASSOCIATION PRESS : NEW YORK

*To Mickie*

*Other Books by Rudolph M. Wittenberg*

# Contents

# Introduction

This book has been written to call to attention a phase of growth in the life cycle that has been largely neglected in both the professional and popular literature. There is between the late teens and the early twenties a specific period that has been called post-adolescence.

The available evidence—from psychological and sociological sources—suggests that post-adolescence is much more difficult to negotiate than is commonly assumed, and that indeed a considerable number of young adults stumble and fall. Some embark on treacherous roads which lead them into serious trouble; others stop growing emotionally and regress to earlier adolescent or childhood behavior. Still others find for themselves pseudo-solutions, which are often dictated by their harsh inner policemen—their rigid superegos—instead of by balanced, mature judgment. They settle for second or third best and enter the mainstream of life with a resigned, lifeless attitude. There are, among young adults, many more suicide attempts than most of us realize and more actual suicides than we care to consider. Young adulthood is a very difficult time for some people.

Some of the problems of post-adolescence are as unavoidable as any growing pain in any phase of life; others may be avoided or modified by a better understanding of young adulthood. Thus, one of the purposes of this book is to detail some of the characteristics of this period, to attempt to show what is happening inside and outside young men and women in their late teens and early twenties.

This knowledge may stimulate the reader to reconsider the whole concept of "coming of age" and help him to recognize that the publicized symptoms of drug addiction, violence, and crime are neither the typical nor the major problems of post-adolescence.

When you work closely with young adults, as I have done over the past twenty-five years both in psychoanalytic practice and as consultant to social agencies and clinics, you are impressed with the gradual breakdown, the leaving of high school and college. Even with the more seriously disturbed young adults we have seen at Elmhurst Hospital in Queens, New York, where I have been a consultant, my students, psychiatric residents, psychological interns, social workers, and nurses were not so much concerned with an occasional acting-out episode as with the lack of direction and the absence of sound values. Parents, counselors, teachers, and clergymen who have been attending my seminars at the New School for Social Research in New York City commented on the badly balanced relationships between young adults, their feelings of isolation and inability to experience life intensely.

Between the faulty assumption that adulthood follows on the heels of adolescence, on the one side, and the culturally condoned prejudice against recognition of problems and using help constructively, on the other, the young adult is caught in a psychological and social bind.

Not only is society discouraging him from facing his problems or asking for help, but even if he did overcome these hurdles, he would be up against another one: who is equipped to help?

Parents have little status with young adults. Teachers, counselors, and clergymen are suspect. And clinicians are considered the absolutely last, desperate resource.

Thus, another purpose of this book is to show that in spite of the suspicions of young adults, there are people who care, and have been able to help them. There are intelligent parents, there are thoughtful teachers, wise counselors, compassionate clergymen, skilled clinicians. For them this book was written.

It begins and ends with fictionalized reports of six real young people to whom reference is made throughout the book. The discussion of their troubles is used to illustrate some theoretical concepts about post-adolescence, then related to possible causes, and finally used to point to some solutions.

Technical terms have been avoided as much as possible, and are employed only where it would have been awkward to try to circumvent them.

To the six young people and all young people whom I have had the privilege to help, to their parents and leaders, my colleagues and friends who have read the manuscript goes my sincere and humble gratitude. If all our efforts will help toward a better understanding of this phase of growth, it will have been worth all the trouble—theirs and mine.

# PART I

# Six Young People

~~

# 1

## Linda Lewis

*"The Woman Beautiful"*

There is no doubt in anybody's mind that Linda has talent. A lot of talent. Her teachers in high school have told her so, and the professional drama coaches with whom she has been studying are quite certain that Linda will make it big one day. She seems to pick up the character of any part she has to play and get into it, almost becoming Juliet or Anna Christie. Memorizing parts is no problem to her, projecting comes naturally, she is a good-looking young actress of eighteen who has decided that she needs summer stock, contact with agents, and walk-on parts in small theaters more than college —although she could have gotten into several colleges, according to her high school guidance counselor.

Not that she looks eighteen. If you saw her walking down Broadway in her blue jeans, her leather boots, and suede jacket, you would take her for twenty easily. The black bangs emphasize her large, dark eyes, which seem even more startling because she is so pale—partly from lack of sleep, partly because Linda does not believe in lipstick, mascara, or any makeup.

She is strictly down on all this stuff. Hates it. Hates anything artificial. Hates policemen, teachers, bus drivers, and a category called "Parents"—Linda hates a lot of different people and things. Not that her kind of hate is visible on contact. On the contrary, she likes to be "nice" and expects other people to be "nice" back. Her contempt for the outside world is expressed in one word that is used to blanket everybody and anything she is against—"Stupid!"

In high school, when she was found wandering in the halls without a pass, her reaction was, "Stupid system!" Getting up for one boring assembly after another was not worth her while, particularly since she had had late rehearsals at the acting studio, and preferred sleeping late. After the truant officer had come and gone, she told her mother that this was a stupid waste of time. When her boy friend's family insisted that he come home by one o'clock on Saturday nights, Linda was very certain that Josh had stupid parents. How can you have a good time at a party, or driving out to a beach picnic, if you have to watch the clock?

Time is another thing Linda hates. Her mother bought her a pretty wristwatch for her seventeenth birthday—a financial sacrifice for a woman bringing up a daughter alone on a bookkeeper's salary —but Linda really didn't see any need for wearing a watch. There are clocks all around you in a big city like New York, and who wants to be reminded of time every minute anyway? All these regulations of time are just as stupid as the worry about money. Going to bed at a definite time, getting up at a definite time, meeting people on the dot of seven—Stupid!

But while she will control her contempt for the world around her, she is very open in her antagonism to boys. She may be willing to admit that she is going too far when she calls the reality around her "stupid," but not when it comes to boys or men. There she will not compromise.

Why? She will tell you if you ask her. She will say quite candidly that sooner or later—more sooner than later—anybody, anything that wears pants, will get around to telling her that she is beautiful, pretty, gorgeous. And if there is one thing Linda hates to hear, it is the fact—and it is a fact—that she is exceptionally attractive. This is the one thing she has heard since she could distinguish words, since earliest infancy, all through the crawling stage into childhood, nursery, and kindergarten, right up to junior high school. By then, she had learned to be so ornery that nobody bothered to tell her. She stopped this effectively.

Her mother, a pleasant but plain-looking woman, could not believe that she had given birth to such perfection, and to this day, she looks at Linda as she would a painting. Long before Linda could determine anything for herself, she was conditioned to exhibit her beauty.

Her curls, her complexion, her big black eyes, were forever a challenge to her mother who bought the cutest dresses, ribbons, and shoes, and paraded her "doll" around the neighborhood, guarding her as if she were a priceless treasure that must not have a scratch, a spot, a wrinkle. Linda looked even more ravishing when she smiled, so that she was urged, encouraged, badgered, to smile at anybody who happened along.

By the second year of her life, Linda was so conditioned to smile and move in what the adults considered "cute" manners that she did it automatically, learning to turn it off and on. Getting all smeared up with a piece of candy, or rolling in the wet sand by the beach, was considered a major tragedy, so that Linda learned to sit still and do as little as possible since any activity was bound to get her into trouble.

To the mother, who lost her husband when Linda was barely two, this beautiful child became the most important achievement of her life, the one focus around which her own life revolved. Linda easily won the beautiful baby contests, and was slated to be a model long before she entered kindergarten. It was a foregone conclusion that she was to make her way as "The Woman Beautiful."

In kindergarten she discovered that she was also a human being. The teacher hung up all the children's drawings without names on them—they had been penciled on with an explanation on the back —and on Visitors' Day, people chose Linda's as one of three to be awarded a box of lollipops. Linda was more bewildered than pleased at first, because she knew that it was her work that had been judged, not her appearance.

To be recognized for her achievements, rather than for what nature had given her, became increasingly important. She tried out her abilities in many little ingenious ways, always with the aim to discover what she was really like, independent of her physical beauty. She would offer to help her classmates with compositions and make them swear an oath not to reveal the author of the work. The children were only too glad to have an able friend do their work for them, which invariably was returned with high marks.

Linda loved group tests, where numbers instead of names were used for identification. When she lagged in her own homework and got report cards with average marks, her mother assured her that this did not matter very much, since in the work she would be doing —modeling and the stage—intelligence was not that important. Linda reacted to this by redoubling her academic efforts and bringing her marks up to the top. She did all she could to play down her appearance, but if some newcomer innocently told her how pretty she was, Linda would either withdraw into icy silence or get downright nasty. To be called beautiful was about the last thing in the world she wanted. It meant being used for Mother's gratification, to be promoted and packaged like a piece of merchandise.

When the young people in her second year of high school were encouraged to volunteer in community work during the summer vacation, Linda chose working with blind children. She was a faithful volunteer, reading and dramatizing stories for the children with her expressive voice, arranging ingenious games, and singing songs to them, teaching them to participate, and bringing joy and laughter into the darkness of these children who had no eyes to behold her beauty.

It was in the day camp for blind children that she met Josh, the boy who accompanied the children to the park and beach with her. A very timid, frightened boy, Josh would never have dared to put his adoration of Linda into words, and instead, expressed his affection by being always at her side, carrying out her every wish, and making the work as easy as possible—carrying the heavier packages of lunch and drink, offering his strength, his better muscles, to ease her job. It was Linda who took the initiative in their relationship by being flirtatious in a playful way, telling him not to be so serious, and suggesting the first date with the excuse that Josh was getting too somber about life and should have some fun.

This was the only way in which she was able to have relationships with boys, and Josh was one of the few boys she could accept. She was the dominant force from the start, and this was the only way the two could exist together. Linda determined when they were to meet, where they were to go, what movies or plays they were to see. She also determined his behavior, his clothes, his initiative—managing him the same way in which she had been managed by her mother. After she had picked out a shirt or tie for him, she would tell him how handsome he looked, how cute he was, and how pleased she was with him. Josh was her child, and she played the role of the mother in the only way she had known it.

Josh had never excited her or stimulated her fantasies. She took care of him and protected him against his "stupid" parents, while sexual feelings were directed against an older girl in acting class, to whom she found herself strongly attracted. When this tall, masculine young woman put her arms around Linda, she felt highly stimulated and protected.

What drew Linda and this older girl—let's call her Anita—together, was their feelings of contempt for men. Where Linda considered men stupid for the silly admiration of her attractiveness —of which she had no inkling herself—Anita had always actively competed with boys, and later, with men, certain that "anything you can do, I can do better." She felt vastly superior to men and treated them as if they were playthings. She never took a man seriously or respected him because, to her, the whole male species was second-rate.

Linda, who had been treated as a plaything, first by her mother and then by many boys, and therefore had not been able to develop much respect for her own femininity, was excited and warmed to have found an older girl who saw the female as the ultimate in creation, and who taught her that men were not to be taken seriously. Anita's interest was safe, as far as Linda was concerned, almost as safe as that of the blind children. Since she was a woman herself, one did not have to suspect her of wanting anything except genuine love for her personality. Linda looked up to Anita, allowed her to guide her, to help her with her studies in the theater, to advise her on what to wear, whom to trust.

When Linda's mother objected to Linda's short haircut, her plain clothes, her staying out late with Anita, the mother-daughter relationship disintegrated completely, to the point where Linda moved in with Anita. Her admiration for Anita and the older girl's ideas did not stop at the intellectual level. Linda also loved Anita's way of walking and moving, she admired her breasts and her whole body. Nothing seemed more desirable than to be close to these breasts and to be held by these arms. Their kisses became passionate, and quite naturally developed into a lesbian relationship.

This became the one aspect of her life that was not "stupid," that made sense. Instead of feeling embarrassed and self-conscious in the company of men who looked at her with admiration or desire, Linda felt superior to them, condescending about their superficial view of women. She would smile at their passes, considering their compliments insults, and in time learned to express her contempt in cutting phrases, which invariably produced a shock effect on the male admirers, much to the amusement of Anita, who would hear about these silly men.

Linda became more sure of herself, walked with more determination, spoke up with more assurance. In the theater, she did particularly well with parts where girls appear disguised as men (as Rosalind, in *As You Like It*), as well as tomboy parts, like Puck, or parts of very young girls. One of her favorite parts, for which she studied a very long time, was Joan of Arc, which she eventually played with excellent notices. She found it comfortable to identify with a young peasant girl of great loyalty and devotion who went on with great determination to carry out her mission, leading men in battle and never once using her femininity to accomplish her ends. She talked and acted like men did, and the fact that she was a female seemed to play no part in her conception of the role. That Joan survived as a saintly victim fitted well into Linda's concept of herself, a fanatical young woman who perishes because the world does not understand her.

Once we recall that the world in the beginning of life is the mother—the representative of the world outside—Linda's concept of herself becomes more comprehensible. She had, throughout childhood, felt that she was being used, her attractiveness exploited, instead of being understood and loved as a human being.

The crucial turn of events in her young adult life came when she began to suspect that Anita—the woman she loved—too was beginning to use her. Anita, whose hostility toward men had made her increasingly unpopular in her office, where she had been the manager, lost her job; shortly afterward, while hunting for new employment, she became ill with an old-standing asthma, which now prevented her from talking freely, handicapping her employment possibilities severely.

It now fell to Linda to help with the rent and food expenses, a task for which she was in no way ready. While her mother had given her a small amount toward sharing an apartment with her girl friend, Linda had earned only a few dollars here and there, with walk-on parts, baby-sitting, filling in with odd hours in a telephone-answering service.

Anita expected Linda to take on responsibility for her and the apartment, as she had done for Linda; the older girl became resentful at the younger's declarations of helplessness. If Linda could not help financially, she should take the larger share of the housework. Linda shopped and cooked, cleaned and washed—while Anita became more critical of her performance. The meals were unsatisfactory, the food budget too high. Anita became testy, sharply critical, hostile. Linda, unable to give up the relationship, cried herself to sleep and desperately tried to please her friend, with less and less success.

Leaving their home and returning to Mother was a major defeat for Linda, particularly since her mother, completely unaware of the nature of the relationship, talked marriage to her. It was quite understandable, Mother said, for a young girl to want to live away from home and share an apartment with a girl friend, but sometimes such things do not work out. Linda should not be so blue about it and instead, should begin to think of establishing her own home, marrying, settling down, and having a family.

Since Linda was unable to tell her mother anything about Anita and her sexual involvement with her, the mother took the daughter's tight-lipped silence as a sign of conformity and penance. Linda is beginning to see the light, she will find a nice young man and be happy again. You are very pretty, Mother repeated. If you stop wearing these rags your girl friend talked you into, you can go anywhere and have any man you like.

Linda, subdued and down in the mouth, got a great deal of attention in the theater, where people were solicitous, and tried to cheer her up. It did not help much, particularly since her flat and distant behavior had begun to show in her acting and to be noticed by the leading people around her. Some parts that seemed to be natural for her went to other students, and there was less enthusiasm about her performances, leaving her feeling realistically discouraged.

Nobody had any solutions for her unhappy state, except Mother, who kept talking marriage as the natural way of happiness for any girl.

Linda would not hear of any such thing, but she had no answer that seemed better. Slowly, she went along with her mother's plans for meeting eligible young men and, in spite of her hate and deep feelings of revulsion for him, she married one of the young, well-to-do men who had been enchanted by her beauty. She looked beautiful in her bridal gown, and was photographed for several magazines.

This venture lasted six months, ending in divorce and leaving Linda with enough money to have a small place of her own. She works as a receptionist in a downtown advertising agency and spends two evenings a week at the theater school. On weekends, she cleans her apartment, goes shopping, and occasionally sees a movie. Some weekends she visits Joshua, who now is married and has a little baby. She is neither terribly unhappy nor ever very buoyant.

Without attempting any clinical discussion of this complex young woman, we can certainly understand that Linda has in no way resolved her homosexual dilemma and cannot, on the other side, accept a love relationship with a man. While she does not suffer acute pain most of the time, she knows that something inside is preventing her from getting close to people—young men and young women—so that she lives virtually in emotional isolation.

Instead of resolving the internal conflicts—reaching back to the earliest symbiotic tie to her mother and their hostile dependency relationship—Linda is covering up her empty life with continuous, short-lived activities which satisfy her for brief moments.

A young woman of not even twenty-one years, Linda has her whole life ahead of her—with her lovely face and her healthy body, with a good deal of talent and ambition. That she most likely will not know what to do with herself in years to come is a tragic waste of a troubled young adult.

# 2

# Tom Tibbett

### *"Young Man With Principles"*

The Tibbetts were Methodists, but Tom was not sure what he should call himself. He had attended four different churches during his growing-up years because his father's work had forced him to move around quite a bit. A gifted electronics engineer with two original inventions to his credit, Mr. Tibbett had been recognized and promoted, but almost every promotion brought a move to a different town.

Tom had not minded these travels as much as had his older brother, who formed close ties very slowly and always felt torn up by his roots when the family started packing. Tom was more easygoing. He adjusted to the different schools and churches quite easily and, like his mother, took part in the activities of the community as soon as the family was settled. There was always an outlet for his energies, either in the Grange, the 4-H Club, or the young peoples' group in whatever church came closest to the Tibbetts. His excellent academic record followed him from school to school, and to nobody's surprise, Tom made early admission in one of the outstanding Ivy League colleges.

No sooner was he settled in his new school—registered, program card in hand, dormitory assigned—when he made his way to the tennis courts just outside campus, where he was asked for a game of doubles in no time.

Tom was like that—personable, pleasant, and obviously bright. People took to him right away. He found a new girl friend in the nearby girls' college, but kept up his correspondence with several girls whom he had liked in the past. The fellows considered Tom a regular guy, even though there were a few dissenters who suspected him of being square at times. Tom would not cheat on exams nor would he let others copy his homework, and no matter at what time the gang got home Saturday night, he would insist on getting up Sunday morning for church. When he came late to the football game because he had not finished his homework, and when he refused a double date because he had not written to his family that week, the dissenters passed the word that Tibbett was definitely a square or almost a plain chump, the term usually reserved for teachers.

Tom was not terribly bothered by the opinions of this particular group, and instead drifted toward one of the other groups on campus, the circle of principled, responsible young people who took the initiative in school and community affairs. Because he was able and eager to contribute, he was given a great many responsible jobs in the youth organizations.

The committees would meet and get through their business of inviting speakers and planning forums fairly quickly, but when it came to writing to the guests, arranging for the hall, seeing to it that chairs were set up, microphone in order, loudspeaker connected, Tom usually was the one who could be counted on to actually do it. Although the jobs were beginning to pile up and encroach on his study time, Tom was not able to enlist enough responsible people to distribute the chores evenly. Students began to count on him, and instead of relieving him of some of his burdens, elected him secretary one term, president another, editor a third—with the result that Tom became known as the voice of the student body. At the same time, his academic work began to suffer, his very high marks dropping slightly, not enough to make him concerned, but sufficiently to warrant the attention of his adviser.

Professor Weston did not specially call him in, but used the monthly review of the student paper as an opportunity to talk to Tom, who, as editor, was the one to meet with faculty anyway.

The editorial, which Tom himself had written, defended the students' rights to invite a controversial speaker for the monthly forum. It was a well-reasoned argument, carefully phrased, politely but firmly stating the students' position which was known to be in opposition to some sections of the faculty and a minority of the regents.

The adviser himself, though he had not made it widely known to the student body, was thoroughly in sympathy with what he called the First Amendment Position of the student paper's editorial board. He fully believed that the young people had the right, even the duty, to listen to anybody who wanted to be heard, regardless of his persuasion. He wanted discussion of controversial issues and welcomed Tom's stand.

Tom, however, went into the conference with a defensive attitude, expecting the usual administrative criticism and expression of restraint, a lecture on the difference between freedom and license, with the result that he was not ready to hear what his adviser had to say.

"There will be some fireworks, Tom," he said, "and maybe your popularity will suffer a bit. Do you mind that?"

He had chosen a personal trail, since he was more concerned with Tom than the editorial.

Tom, misunderstanding his professor, assured him that he was not concerned with himself, but with the principle. He could not worry about the welfare of Tom Tibbett continuously, but had to sacrifice, if necessary, for the greater good.

"I'm with you in principle," his professor assured Tom, "but can't this matter of sacrifice be carried too far where it becomes self-destructive, when for example it affects your marks?"

Tom was not ready to face this complex and basic issue, and tried to treat it lightly. He was, he assured his adviser, still in the tenth percentile of his class and on the dean's list. He doubted that his community activities had any bearing on his scholarship. Could the professor, please, discuss the editorial instead?

"I think it's fine," Professor Weston assured a surprised Tom, and ended the conference, sensing that the student was not ready for more at the moment.

A few weeks later, however, the same conflict came up again when a delegation of students volunteered to participate in the sit-in demonstrations in town, where a number of restaurants had refused to serve Negroes. Tom actively participated in this delegation and recruited quite a few members into it. The action involved picketing the restaurants, sitting at the counter with Negro students until they would be served, facing a hostile crowd and a battle with the police.

This was the first night of many to come in which Tom did not get his seven hours' rest; he overslept his first class the next morning. He was not the only one; the whole delegation had been so upset and disturbed by the violence on the picket line—one demonstrator had had to be hospitalized—that they sat up most of the rest of the night discussing the incident, airing their conflicting views and planning new strategy.

Keenly aware of the effect community activities could have on his schoolwork, Tom made doubly sure to have his assignments in on time, to finish all the assigned reading, to write up the lab experiments—but no more. He did exactly and precisely what was required, and this he did with sheer discipline and determination, not with love for or deep interest in the work. His heart, as the saying goes, was no longer in it.

What concerned him deeply was the world outside school—civil rights battles, political controversies, the stand churches took on issues of worldwide significance. His good mind, his able word, were increasingly put to use in large, controversial issues. Some things were just plain wrong to him, and he was in no mood to compromise with evil. He had no patience with delaying tactics, avoidance, and procrastination. That his fellow students could not get a cup of coffee in any diner in town was wrong. That his Catholic colleagues defended restrictions or a ban on birth control was intolerable to him in the face of the rapid population increase and the fact that in large areas of the world, people were starving. He pulled no punches in his debates and insisted on being equally frank and bold in his editorials. He wrote to senators protesting nuclear explosions, commercial use of public highways, and the neglect of national parks. He read continually and quickly, and retained the salient facts so that he could debate with facts and figures.

When his group took a public stand on the threatened dismissal of a professor, Tom got into the newspapers, and this was the first time his parents heard about his activities. He had written home as usual, mentioned schoolwork, his marks, some of his friends, and sports, but had not discussed his newly found public interests.

Mr. Tibbett did not like his son's image, and announced his

forthcoming visit in no uncertain terms, while his mother assured him in a footnote that she was with him in whatever he undertook.

In the meantime, the school administration had taken steps to stop the students' public support for the threatened teacher, and when the young people refused to heed the school's warnings, the administration called in the police to stop the demonstrations. There were some arrests, after a tussle with the police, and Tom was scheduled for a court hearing by the time his father arrived.

Cautioned by his wife, Tom's father made it a point to see Tom's adviser first to try to understand his son's behavior. Professor Weston spoke about Tom with warmth and empathy, but left no doubt in Mr. Tibbett's mind that his son was in trouble. No doubt about it. It was difficult to predict, he said, what the next developments would be, but certainly Tom was not the same able, ambitious student who had come to the school on early admission.

Mr. Tibbett, in defense, offered the example of his older son, who had just received a teaching fellowship toward his master's degree with a sizable public health grant. Both boys had had the same upbringing, Mr. Tibbett pleaded; there was no preference of one over the other, and he was completely at a loss to understand what had turned Tom into a maverick, if not a rebel.

Professor Weston tried to assure the worried father that some of the finest minds pass through such phases and suggested that there was really nothing wrong with Tom's line of development, since it was consistent and, in a way, a continuation of a vigorous involvement in community activities.

Mr. Tibbett got no comfort from the adviser's explanations and suggested that the school take some responsibility in getting his son back on the right track. He intimated that since these radical developments did not originate in Tom's home, they had to be caused in some way by the new environment, the friends he had chosen and the school itself. Professor Weston promised to do what he could to be of help to Tom, but he was not certain that he had that much influence over his students.

Tom's mother, in the meantime, had visited with her son in his room and listened with admiration to the report of his activities. As far as she was concerned, Tom was doing what he thought was right, and this was all she wanted him to do. She cautioned him about his father's distress and deep concern, but again assured him of her support.

When Mr. Tibbett, in his talk with Tom, blamed the school for the trouble the son had gotten into, the young man sharply disagreed and insisted on taking the full responsibility for his actions. His father, however, was equally adamant, and demanded that Tom think of transferring to the school near home, where the family could keep in closer contact with their youngest, "emotionally disturbed," son. A few discussions with the minister in town should be of great help to Tom.

Tom had no objections to seeing the minister, whom he had liked for many years, but he declared in polite, firm language that he saw no indication of emotional disturbance whatsoever. Was he not out of step with society? his father asked, and Tom had to agree that he was in opposition to much that was going on around him. This did not mean, however, that there was anything wrong with him, but with certain parts of society! Society needed a doctor, not Tom Tibbett.

To his surprise, his mother, who had consistently been on his side, now sounded a note of caution. The world was in trouble, she assured Tom, but was there not something wrong with him too if his career was about to be wrecked? Had he not talked about going into medicine, or the ministry, and how was he going anyplace if he used up most of his energy in public battles?

Tom thought that his mother sounded like his adviser now, and for a moment got the feeling there was a conspiracy of the adult world against him, against youth. Perhaps his friends, who swore that people over thirty should not be trusted, were right after all. A whole long line of familiar arguments came conveniently to mind— Two different generations can never see eye to eye. The adults made this world, and how can they see how bad it is? Parents and teachers have a vested interest in the *status quo*—generalizations so broad that they, like certain quotations, could be used to prove anything.

When his father asked for a definite commitment, a sharp restriction in his "extracurricular activities," with the threat of withdrawal of financial support to back it up, Tom had to agree, feeling that he was a victim of the establishment, the people who control the purse strings.

A very short time after this meeting, Tom started to grow a beard and to gain weight. It was almost as if his physical image had to change, since he could not discharge his rebellion in social action. When his current girl friend asked him why he had not tried to stay in school on a scholarship, Tom assured her that with his reputation as a troublemaker, he would never have gotten such a grant. The other alternative, to study back home, was completely out of the question. He was certain that he could never again live or work near home, which to him now meant the seat of the settled, the calcified, the reaction.

When he filled out a questionnaire the following term indicating his major field of study, he wrote "sociology" instead of "medicine" or "the ministry." He explained to his girl friend, who now was becoming more and more important in his life, that he could continue most of his social action interests "legitimately" by becoming a sociology major. Field trips down south, help with voter registration, could all be classified as part of studying sociology.

At the same time, he secretly envied two of his friends who had gone ahead with the "pre-med" program, were deeply involved in biology and chemistry, and considered Tom's studies with just a trace of condescension. Almost as if to prove to himself that he was on the right track, Tom distanced himself from his former classmates, used his field trips as a basis for an honor paper, and got much recognition for this from the school.

While the manifest conflict between Tom and his family and school had been resolved to some degree, his inner conflicts had increased. Although he hardly ever admitted this to himself, the study of sociology did not challenge him as much as he had hoped. He missed the precision and elegance of a mathematical proof, the definiteness of chemical formulas, the rigor of the natural sciences. It was, he would say to his girl friend, almost too easy, and not "scientific" enough. The young lady, who was concerned with nursery-school education, assured him that he was on the right track, in spite of his feelings, and encouraged him to go ahead, particularly since he was doing so very well.

Tom found himself troubled, however, by his lack of commitment to his studies, his lack of real contact with his family—the correspondence had become reduced to newsy items and gossip, instead of the former vigorous exchange of ideas—the estrangement from his former adviser, whom he had had to give up together with his change of major.

The need to be close to somebody, to belong, to be accepted—since he accepted himself less than before—increased to the point where he seriously considered marrying the young nursery-teacher student.

Two events during the following year precipitated a development that was to become permanent for Tom. A local research outfit that had been looking for a young sociologist on a part-time basis offered him some money, and at the same time his girl friend told him that she was afraid she was pregnant.

Tom, at this juncture, used a vacation trip home to see his minister for several long discussions. The young man did not hide his doubts about the field he found himself involved in, his doubts about a married life and the responsibility for a family. He did talk about some physical symptoms—a great need for sleep, a frequent state of tiredness, a lack of energy. The minister tried to understand Tom, particularly in relation to his girl friend, and suggested that he consult his family physician for his physical ills. The doctor put him through the standard tests, checked all the vital organs, ran the chemical tests—and gave him a clean bill of health. Physically, Tom was in excellent shape—no vitamin deficiency, no anemia, no lowered blood pressure, to account for the state of tiredness, no pathology in any of the vital organs; in brief, no findings.

Tom went back once again to his minister and confessed that he was very disappointed by the physician's report. He would rather be sick than go on suffering from this unexplained and draining lack of energy.

Apparently, the minister suggested, Tom was burdened down psychologically, worried about his girl friend, his professional choice, his way of life. Tom readily agreed that he was very worried about Janet, but if she were pregnant—and there would be certainty about this in a few weeks—he saw no alternative but to marry her and start his family.

To his surprise, the minister did not consider this the only alternative. He sounded to Tom like his old adviser when he cautioned that raising a family now, particularly if he were not sure he loved Janet, might be too much for Tom. While such a step would relieve some of the guilt, there was a major question about their future and that of a child whom neither parent perhaps wanted. Should the possibility of offering the child for adoption through a responsible agency not also be considered? There were, he assured Tom, many couples who had an established, solid marital foundation who were very eager to adopt a child. A reliable social agency would thoroughly check such a family before they would consider offering them the child; would this solution not perhaps be wiser in the long run for all concerned? Tom, who had never thought of such a step, looked a little less glum when he left the minister, feeling that he was not completely trapped, and might have some free choices in his life.

He had not told his family anything about the current crisis, but his girl friend, who had gone home during the vacation, had been unable to hide her fears from her mother, who had suspected pregnancy from the usual early symptoms. Janet assured her family that she and Tom had planned to get married anyway, and simply would do it now, instead of three months later. The mother made contact with Tom's family by asking about the wedding arrangements, and with this, the family pressures ground into motion, determining every single step in Tom's development from that point on. Feeling very liberal and generous for not chiding Tom or Janet, both families chained the young people down with a heavy burden of gifts, kindness, and generosity.

At the request of Tom's parents, the minister performed the ceremony. There was a small, pleasant wedding, and both families helped the young people set up their own home.

Tom experienced all this as though it were not Tom Tibbett, but somebody else getting married and setting up a home and family. With his old discipline and intelligence, he succeeded in going through all the new and unfamiliar steps without causing any unpleasantness or difficulty.

The time when he could not use his controls, and looked aghast at the situation was at night. He frequently woke up now with unexplained nightmares, strange combinations of events and people, that left him lying awake for hours. During the day he was more tired than before. Although he had shaved off his beard at the request of both families, he was unable to control his desire to eat and drink. He put on more and more weight and moved with the sluggishness and hesitation of burdened-down people. The old feeling that the cards were stacked against him had become very dominant. He believed that he had to be constantly on his guard, trust nobody, and avoid close contact with people. This included his wife and little child, his parents, and Janet's family.

Although he did not see any point in it, he finished school and took a job as a polltaker for a market research outfit. The company likes his work but wishes Tibbett had more motivation for the job. He is doing just what he has to, and no more. Janet has the same complaint. His mother, too, wonders what ever became of Tom's promise and fire. He sounds and moves like an old man, at the age of twenty.

There will be many who would not consider Tom as a young man in trouble. And compared to some young people he is not antisocial, not dangerous to society, nor to himself. He is, however, a very gifted human being who is not likely to fulfill his many potentials unless he gets some help. Functioning in a low key, merely existing in a state of mild depression at the much heralded age of maturity, is not a state of good health. In a very different sense than Linda and the other young people, Tom Tibbett, too, is a youth in trouble.

# 3

# Gwen Grant

## *"I Can't Do It"*

Like so many other young people, Gwen didn't show her troubles until she was past sixteen. Her mother said that Gwen had changed practically overnight, or at least within a few months. "Can't imagine what got into the girl," Mrs. Grant said. "After all this time, you'd think a nice-looking, smart kid like Gwen would know better than to make a fool of herself."

She used to be nice and helpful, both at home and with the neighbors. Back on the old country road, where the Grants lived on their small farm—Mr. Grant was a logger, but worked in the mill whenever he got a chance—in their little settlement, Gwen was known as the kid you could always count on when you needed a hand. Even as a tiny tot, she got along with the other kids; when it came to playing house, she would take the part of the baby because nobody else wanted it, and after all, she was the baby at home with two older sisters and one married brother. Gwen should know how to play the baby.

But not only in games; in work, too, she was always the same good kid. Gathering kindling wood for the fireplace had been her job since she was five, and it seemed natural to continue this practice when she joined the Girl Scouts and went on cookouts. Neighbors, well aware of her even temperament, gave her baby-sitting jobs and got her to help with chores at spring cleaning; Gwen got pleasure from saving her earnings in her piggy bank. Somehow, the other kids found out that she was a soft touch, and Gwen lent them nickels and dimes because she didn't know how to say No.

When she asked for her money back, the kids laughed at her and claimed never to have borrowed a cent. She lost library privileges because another girl, who had borrowed her card, failed to return books for several weeks.

When Gwen went to her mother with tears in her eyes and complained, Mrs. Grant brushed her off by telling her that she was no longer a baby, and had to watch out for herself. But the trouble was that Gwen still felt like the baby, the youngest member of a large family, and did not quite know how to be herself without trying to please the others.

For a time she hung back and watched other children, trying to learn from them, and just before her fourteenth birthday, she showed what her mother called the Big Change. Gwen got suddenly nasty. She didn't just say No if she didn't want to do something; she used foul language and vulgar gestures, shocking her peers as well as the grown-ups. Her father and big brother had to laugh when the small, skinny kid started swearing like a trooper, and assured Mother and the rest of the family that these things didn't mean much in a girl of her age. She would grow out of it and be herself again.

One of her favorite teachers, too, considered Gwen's ornery talk a passing phase, but was concerned when the intelligent, studious girl started to fail her tests. She made stupid mistakes, almost as if she were daring the teacher to fail her. Gwen seemed to be totally unfamiliar with material she had shown to have mastered throughout the term, when it came to examinations. She did other strange things. After sitting up half the night doing her homework and memorizing, she would forget to take the work to school, and on one or two occasions left it in the school bus.

When, in the middle of the final English examination, her mind went blank once again, Gwen put down her pen and stopped dead. It was no use, she told herself; I can't do it. She lowered her head and sat quietly crying, her hands covering her face. When the teacher came over to her, Gwen did not respond at first, but when the proctor, a young, sympathetic student teacher, kept encouraging her, she suddenly snapped around and yelled at the teacher to leave her alone. She shocked the young teacher and the whole class when she broke into the silent room with a high, strident scream, demanding to be left alone, hating sympathy and all that crap, and why didn't everybody go away and leave her alone?

"Why did you have to make a fool out of yourself?" was what her mother said. "Wasn't it bad enough that you didn't know the work?"

Gwen, without waiting, screamed at her mother, insisting that she had known the work. But Mrs. Grant, unlike the young teacher, responded to the scream with a severe thrashing, ending all further talk.

If the principal had not intervened and gone to considerable trouble, Gwen would never have graduated from high school, but would have been expelled that very year, when similar scenes occurred on several occasions.

There was no more talk about becoming a teacher or a nurse, or becoming anything, because no matter what anybody proposed to Gwen, there were always the same answers: "I can't do it," or, "I don't care."

Feeling like Cinderella with her two older sisters successful and privileged, and considering her mother a hateful witch, Gwen told her married brother—the only one who could talk to her—that she was not going to stay at home any longer. She had tried getting her father to understand her, but gave up when Mr. Grant failed to sense what was troubling her. He was calm and friendly, and assured her that everything would be all right, that Mother didn't mean any harm and that Gwen should have more patience with her poor, overworked mother, who had slaved all her life for her children.

Gwen had made up her mind to leave the old clapboard house on the county road and move to town, where she was certain she could find work, either in the mill or in a restaurant, or someplace. She did not feel happy about the prospect of living alone, but saw no other way.

Finding a place to live, finding a place to work, were strange experiences, because no matter where she went and what she said, all people sounded like Mother and her two sisters. The woman who had a room to rent not only wanted to know all about Gwen over two cups of coffee, but she also insisted that Gwen bring no men visitors and do no cooking in her room. She demanded that Gwen stay for dinner, and was upset when the young woman did not eat anything to speak of. In the settlement on Main Street, where many young women had rooms, it appeared that the other girls had all the good rooms and that only a dark little mansard was left for her. The window looked exactly like the one in her room back home.

The same thing happened when she looked for work. They were not hiring at the textile mill just now, but there were a few signs for waitresses and for salesgirls at Penney's Department Store. Wherever she went, there were always a few girls ahead of her who looked better, sounded smarter, knew more, and looked down at her. She was always the last one, the latecomer, the baby—almost as if things had been planned that way for her. She seemed to be arraigned at the end of a long line, an inevitable, fated situation for which there would never be a solution.

When, standing in the corner of the restaurant where she had finally taken a job, Gwen saw a young man looking in her direction, she turned around to find out which girl he was staring at. There was nobody in the place at the moment, except herself. It was so incredible that she looked again, but the other two girls were in the kitchen waiting for their orders, and the fourth one was off duty. There was no doubt about it then, the man was looking at her, Gwen Grant. She did not know what to make of this. The man must be mistaking me for one of the other girls, she decided, or for somebody who used to work here. There had been, she had been told, a girl working here a year ago who was a dead ringer for her. This is what the man must be looking at—her double.

But the man meant her, and he told her so. It took Gwen a while to let this fact sink in, and then she drew the only possible conclusion from this that made sense to her: the man was off his rocker. With three other girls, better-looking, smarter, more experienced than herself, why would anybody ask *her* for a date? Something had to be wrong with the guy. As she stood and talked with him, she looked him over for telltale signs of his deficiency. He seemed all right at first, but when you looked a little longer, you couldn't help noticing that there was something funny about his hand. She studied the hand and discovered that his forefinger was missing; there was a funny clump near the thumb and, clearly, a stitch mark where the finger should have been. A cripple. Somebody who had had an accident in the mill. There you are. She knew it right away. There had to be something wrong with a man who picked

Gwen Grant. And when he came again and kept on asking her, she noticed something else wrong. The way he talked. Common. Plain. No education. A common laborer who had nothing and was nothing. What do you expect, Gwen Grant?

Because she expected nothing for herself, she would volunteer for the jobs that everybody else avoided; but later she would complain that she was being taken advantage of. The fact that nothing good ever happened to her became permanently established as a part of her character that showed up in small and large aspects of her life. If she took the bus, the good seats all seemed to be taken. When she went to buy a special at the A & P, the choice items had already been sold. The good tippers in the restaurant invariably seemed to choose the other girls' tables.

This is the way the big ball bounces, Gwen decided, and lowered her expectations. When she went to the county fair with the other girls from the restaurant, she sought out the fellows nobody else would look at. As she made a date, and as she went out with a young man, she knew all the time that she didn't like him; she would hate to be kissed by him, but, she told herself, that's all I can expect, and you're supposed to take what you can get. There was always something wrong with her dates; indeed, she chose them because they were not too desirable. When the other girls asked her why she always picked "creeps," she shrugged her shoulders and told them to mind their own business. What did they know?

She did not hide her lack of attraction from the young men, and became known as the tough girl with the sharp tongue. She made sure that nobody trespassed into her inner private world. Petting and making out was OK, as long as the boys got satisfied, but what she would not tolerate was any inquiry into her feelings. Even such an innocuous question as "Penny for your thoughts?" could send her off into a defensive tirade about her privacy. If anybody showed real warmth and loving interest in her obvious misery, Gwen would let him have it with both barrels. None of that gooey lovey-dovey stuff, she would announce in a high and incensed voice; mind your own business and I'll mind mine. She would talk about anything the fellows wanted to talk about—the mill that was moving south because wages were cheaper, the unemployment in town, the flood

control project, elections and foreign policy, religion and movies—
anything at all, as long as it did not get personal.

She wanted nothing from people, and had become self-reliant
with a vengeance. To balance her budget, she had learned to manage on a minimum of food and had become thin and scrawny. To
save on bus fare, she walked briskly, with large steps, her shoulders
drawn together, her head downcast. Because she was a good, reliable worker, she was appreciated on her job and, in time, started to
put a little money in the savings bank. She became concerned about
health and hospitalization insurance, and altogether planned to continue her life in the same style in which she had lived it during her
late teens.

It was her married brother who again became concerned on one
of her monthly Sunday visits, and told her that she was making a
mistake in not planning to get married. He pointed to his own
marriage and his two children, and assured her that she was missing the best of life without having children.

To his surprise, Gwen did not fly off the handle at his suggestion.
Not that she relished the idea of being somebody's wife and having
to sleep with a man night after night—not at all. What really intrigued her was the idea of having children, of being a mother.
The image of herself as somebody's mother brought her as close to
excitement as anything could. She told herself that it was too bad
that you needed a man to have children, that you couldn't do it all
by yourself; she even considered marrying just to have children and
then giving the man the air, but this seemed too far out ever to be
accomplished.

As if she had been waiting for somebody close to give her the
go-ahead sign, Gwen found herself doing many things she had often
half considered, but never actually done. She now would not pass a
group of playing children with a fleeting glance, but would stop to
watch them, or even talk to them. She even went back to the neighbors on the old county road and visited the children for whom she
had baby-sat some years back. The children in the house next door
intrigued her, as did the stores that had baby carriages, baby
dresses, blankets, and comforters in the window. When a pregnant
woman came into the restaurant for dinner, Gwen would stare at

her and, if she were her customer, try to bring her extra-large portions and more milk than she had asked for.

One Sunday, when she was on duty, something happened that upset her, intrigued and bothered her more than any other single event she could recall. It was a warm day in May, and through the open door walked the man with the missing finger, a tiny little girl at his side, barely able to walk. He knew which were Gwen's tables, and sat down, but before he could ask for it, Gwen had brought a little baby seat that fitted over the regular chair, tucked a large napkin into the baby's dress, and handed her a plastic spoon to play with. The man smiled at Gwen, as he had always done, but today, she smiled back for the very first time in all the months he had come to the restaurant to eat.

She told him that she was very surprised to see him with a baby, and cautiously inquired whether it were his. "Sure," the man said. "Ellen and me, we're pals." He had not mentioned his wife, and Gwen thought back to the many times he had made passes at her. She remained upset through his stay, and did not know whether to be furious at the married man for having tried to court her or to ask whether something had happened to the baby's mother. It was the baby who took to Gwen and would not let her go about her business of waiting on the other tables, until the man explained that little Ellen must be glad to have a lady around, because she had been brought up entirely by him since his wife's death right after the child's birth.

Gwen was so nervous the rest of the day that her boss complained—something that had never happened since she had been working there. That night, she was so upset and disturbed that she had trouble falling asleep for many hours, and in the morning she called her brother and asked to see him that evening after work.

Did she have the right, she wanted to know, to take another woman's place, just because she wanted to be a mother and take care of the child, even though she did not love the man? Could such a thing work, and should she tell the man how she really felt? The brother persuaded her that love would come in time, as long as she cared for the man and respected him. It seemed to be a miracle come true, and Gwen should not let it pass her by.

Her brother must have been right, Gwen decided soon after, because as she saw more of the man, she was less and less bothered by his accident or his lack of education and, instead, was more and more warmed by his love for the little girl. He almost sounded like her brother when he told her one evening that he knew she cared more for Ellen than for him, but he was convinced that in time she might learn to appreciate him too. If she were willing, he would like nothing more than to marry her and again have a real family.

Gwen saw herself as the substitute of Ellen's real mother, and tried to live up to the image of a woman she had never known, and whom she pictured in her fantasy as the good mother she felt she herself had never had. Bruce, the father of the child, and now Gwen's husband, made no demands on Gwen, let her run the house, and left the care of Ellen entirely to his new wife.

Gwen needed Bruce to reassure her, for from the start, she felt very unsure of her new role and always asked whether what she was doing were what Ellen's "real" mother would have wanted. She would spend hours washing clothes and ironing for Ellen, and always worried lest her own sisters or mother would come to visit and find a spot on Ellen's dress or her hands, a toy on the floor, or the child failing to behave properly.

In her daily walks with the baby, she anxiously compared her to other children and recorded any "backwardness" on the child's part as her own failure. That some other children walked faster, talked more, responded more quickly, became heavy burdens to Gwen. It was terribly important for her to see Ellen succeed in anything she tried. Nothing less than perfection would do—in appearance, in manner, in intelligence, in cleanliness and obedience to her, and particularly to the father.

That the child's father was easygoing by nature, and thought nothing of letting Ellen smear ice cream all over her starched dress distressed Gwen greatly and made her take on still another burden —the education of Bruce, her new husband and the child's father. If the child failed to say, "Thank you," for a piece of candy, Gwen would keep after her until she gave the required response.

The little child quickly learned to do what her mother wanted, but Gwen could not help but notice that when it came to spontaneous expressions of affection or of distress, Ellen went to her father before she went to her. Again, as in the past, Gwen felt that she was not succeeding, in spite of all her efforts. This sense of failure grew when Ellen had spent a day at the home of Gwen's older sister, who lived on the old county road—in the country—and had a baby of her own. Ellen could not stop babbling on about the aunt, the baby, the geese and ducks, the trees and flowers, and wanted nothing more than to return her visit to Gwen's sister. When Gwen, tortured by her old fears, laughingly asked the child whether she would rather live at the farm with the aunt, Ellen nodded vigorously, leaving no doubt that she would have preferred Gwen's sister to Gwen.

When Gwen found herself on familiar ground, she reacted in the familiar way: she redoubled her efforts, as she had at home, in school, and on her job. She worked to get the little child's love and admiration by anticipating her every wish, by never saying No, by giving her whatever she wanted. People told Gwen that she was spoiling the child, and would soon have trouble with her, but she was certain that there was nothing wrong with Ellen, that all the fault was with herself.

The child did sense very soon that she could get anything she wanted from her mother, and made continuous demands, all of which were met, with the result that more demands were made—the beginning of an endless race between Gwen and the growing child, who soon considered her mother as somebody who never said No, and whom she could manipulate the way she pleased.

The child wanted to help her mother, but Gwen felt much too guilty to permit any cooperation and, instead, worked so hard and so continuously that people wondered why she was making herself a slave of her husband and child, from whom she got no thanks for all her efforts.

At twenty, Gwen is an underweight, overworked young woman who can be seen any time scrubbing floors on her knees, doing laundry, lugging heavy bundles, and saving household money to buy a pretty dress for Ellen or a new sweater for her husband. She never buys anything for herself, pays no attention to her appearance, her clothes, or her health, and lives only to serve Ellen and Bruce.

If you'd ask her why she does this, she would tell you that she does not matter, and that she is glad if she can make somebody else happy. She is perfectly sincere when she says, "I don't count."

She seems to be miserable and without any hope; however her expression, "I don't count," is as common as it is deceptive and complex. What she seems to be saying is, "I exist only in relation to somebody else"—the little girl, her husband—as though her own existence were bound up with the existence of somebody else.

This need to live through another person points to a clinically well-known early disturbance in the mother-child relationship, hinting at Gwen's own infantile disturbances. She is of course not at all conscious of these very early traumata, but since she desperately wants to be a better mother than her own mother had been, Gwen will do anything to be as adequate as possible. She will even consider facing her own early disturbances, once she recognizes that they interfere with the little girl's happiness. She will discover that she indeed does count when she is at the point where she seeks professional help.

# 4

# Mark Metcalf

### "Make-out Man"

Mark is going on twenty. Handsome, with a gentle face and smiling blue eyes. He lives in a two-story suburban house with his parents and his ten-year-old sister, Lucy. Mr. Metcalf is in the printing business; his wife, a former schoolteacher, subs now and then, but is always there when the kids get home from school.

If you'd met Mark at a party, or in the clothing store where he works on Saturdays, you would swear that he is the typical "clean-cut, square-jawed, crew-cropped, wholesome American young man." Polite and soft-spoken, he helps old ladies across the street and never talks back to his elders. He is clean, in fact, immaculate in his appearance, and dresses always with an accent on the latest styles. Clothes are his one weakness, he will tell you. He has five sport jackets, at least a dozen pairs of slacks, loads of button-down shirts, and a few ascots. To see one of his friends dressed up in flashy clothes can make him angry. A herringbone tweed with brown brogues for him, no sporting boots and zany belted suits. The idea is not to look like a teen-ager. Metal-studded leather jackets, commodore caps, and tight pants are for punks, not for a mature young man like Mark Metcalf.

What is he going to do when he grows up? He will tell you frankly that he's not sure. Maybe teach English (in college, of course, not public school because the pay is better and it has more status) maybe write books, novels maybe, or stories, or if everything else fails, he can always go into Dad's printing business. Mark's got it made. He is not going to worry about a thing now while he is young and handsome, and can't keep track of the girls that call him every night. Right now, Mark is taking twelve credits at the junior college near home. Three are in subjects like music appreciation (he has always liked listening to records, and his dad has a nice collection of classical records), and two are in speech, where you only have to prepare a little talk every once in a while, and otherwise can have a good time.

He has always been that way, his mother will tell you. He never came right out and said No. He just didn't do it. Perhaps he is a smooth operator, after all, from way back. Lucy, his sister, is the opposite. She works hard, studies until all hours, brings home excellent grades, and fights with Mark because she adores him and can't get under his skin. If you ask Mark, he will tell you with a wink that his little sister has to study because she's not exactly beautiful. As far as he is concerned, good-looking people don't have to work hard. They are privileged by nature. He knows all about having a high "potential" and low performance. He has heard that one ever since junior high school, but it has never cut any ice with him. He even once considered forming a "High Potential Club" at Winston High, but his friend and benefactor, the assistant principal, dissuaded him from this plan.

The line under his picture in the yearbook reads "Make-out Man," and Mark takes pride in this appelation. He will tell you that he is following his parents' wishes not to get serious with any girl right now, but to know many girls. He does know a great many girls, and he is very sure not to be serious with any of them, if for no other reason than that he wouldn't know how. Feeling up girls, undressing them, and sleeping with them is a sport with Mark, as drag racing is with one of his friends, or surfboarding with another. It's fun. That's really all. And what is supposed to be wrong with it? That two of his former girl friends got pregnant and had to get frantic trying to find an abortionist was not Mark's fault, as far as he is concerned. True enough, he has half the responsibility, but no more. In one case, he will tell you, the girl lied when she told him that she was using a diaphragm; in the other case it was an accident. He is sincerely sorry, and will not go near these girls again because, "They're trouble, man."

His parents? Well, Mr. Metcalf will tell you that Mark is really a good boy in his heart. True, he is not very serious, and laughs all his troubles away, but then you're young only once. At twenty you shouldn't have the weight of the world on your shoulders. That will come later. Too interested in girls is one of Mark's problems, girl-crazy, but is there really any harm in it? He could have done better in high school, but some youngsters learn later in life, you know. "I didn't get interested in my work until I was almost thirty," Mr. Metcalf says. "Mark will find his way."

His mother has no real objections to Mark, except when he fights with his little sister. She wants him to lay off Lucy and not get so nasty with her when she borrows his tennis racket or takes a piece of his candy. Mother wishes he would read more, and has brought home lots of paperbacks, good books too, and Mark, to please her, has started to read about ten of them, but lost interest halfway through and put them down. They all seemed to be boring, he said, and since he didn't have to read them for school or any-thing like that, he didn't finish them. Too long.

His boss says Mark is a willing worker. Customers like him. He will put things back in the wrong place sometimes, but if you point it out to him, he will correct his mistakes without any back talk. In fact, he is very polite and apologizes for mistakes right away. You can't get mad at him. He doesn't watch the clock, doesn't in-sult customers who come only to look, doesn't argue with difficult people who want to see the whole stock—Mark is a fine boy, and, as far as his boss is concerned, Mark can have a job anytime he wants. Full-time or part-time.

Mark refuses to worry. About anything. "No point in worrying," he says. When his father had a heart attack, Mark walked around on tiptoe and took the garbage out without being told, and never once asked for the family car. He was polite, as usual, and consid-erate, but he lost no sleep over his father's being in the hospital. He visited him and brought him magazines, and helped his mother. But it did not stop him from doing what he did any day.

If you'd asked him how he felt about his father, he would have told you that he was sorry, and hoped his father would be well again soon. And that is about how he really feels. About his father, his mother, his sister, the girls he sees, the boys he plays basketball with, his teachers, his boss, his minister—anybody. The truth is that Mark does not feel much about anything or anybody. He cares a great deal about his clothes, his shirts, his shoes, and his face. Looking good means something to him. Getting involved with people is one thing Mark cannot do, so that he cannot form real relationships with people, although he considers himself very popular. He is, in fact, isolated from getting close to anybody or investing more than casual feelings in any activity or person—male or female, young or old.

To Mark, the world is a mirror in which he sees himself reflected. He does not really see anybody besides himself. He looks, but he does not see. He hears, but he does not take in what is being said. He does not care, because he does not know how. And this means he is a young man in trouble. The biggest trouble is that he doesn't know he is in it. Nothing can touch him very much, so that your talking to him doesn't make much of an impression, even though he will answer you intelligently and say, "Yes sir, I understand."

In a way he was lucky to have accepted that camp job as swimming counselor last summer because it was there that he got himself into clear and visible trouble, a step which got him to consider the fact that all was not well with him.

For a few days, the job was fun. He stood by the pier, bronzed, muscular, and the target of all the young girls in camp. Helping the kids with swimming, blowing the whistle for "All out," and getting along. There was, of course, one girl who was determined to get him, and succeeded without too much trouble. The camp director, used to flirtations among his staff, watched Mark, whose number he had had from the start, and on two occasions cautioned him to act his age and be aware of his responsibility. There was a definite rule forbidding counselors' leaving camp with campers after hours, aside from the unwritten law prohibiting staff to make dates with campers.

Mark watched his step, particularly remembering his two unfortunate experiences with girls back home, and stayed away from trouble for several weeks. Then came the rainy ten days.

Not only was there no swimming, but there was very little to do for a young man like Mark, who had no inner resources, and was not able to have fun except by playing around with girls. Since this was against the camp rules, Mark found himself bored. He would get dressed in his good-looking sport shirts, sit in the lounge, and leaf aimlessly through magazines.

There were discussions all around him. Since two of the counselors had spent the preceding summer down south helping with voters' registration, they had a great many challenging and interesting stories to tell, which became the target of other counselors. For several days, off and on, a lively, sometimes vigorous civil rights debate was underway. Mark heard what was being said, took the side of first one party, then another, but never more than for the moment. He could not get very excited about any of this, since he was unable to get involved.

There were chess players and Scrabble players; there were the jazz versus the avant-garde music factions, both fighting for their sides to be heard on the one available turntable in the counselors' lounge. Mark was not in any group, nor out of any group; he was, as one of the older staff members said, "out of it." Card playing would hold his interest for brief moments, but even this started to bore him shortly.

The boys in his cottage looked to him for leadership, but he was not able to make suggestions or stimulate the youngsters in any direction. He became known as the counselor who always said, "It's up to you," which the campers shortly recognized was not permissiveness or an invitation to originality, but an expression of indifference. They told him that he did not care, and Mark did not bother to deny it. If the bunk would come up with ideas, Mark would vote with the majority or just sit back, and some of the boys complained that Mark was getting "awful grouchy." The polite and friendly exterior began to peel, cracks appeared in the facade, and hostility came out more openly—hostility which had been hidden since early childhood.

To counteract his feelings of isolation and mild depression, Mark resorted to the only stimulation he knew, sexual play. He disregarded the known dangers of getting caught with the older girls who had chased him and went ahead, repeating what he had always considered the only worthwhile pleasure in his life. To assuage his guilt, he made sure to tell the girl that he did not love her and was not serious, as though this declaration could serve as an alibi against potential future claims. To the girl, his detachment became not a deterrent, but a challenge, inviting more daring and intimate sexual games.

As though he wanted to be caught, Mark played for higher stakes, stayed out after hours, took the girl into a deserted shack near camp, took on another girl—until the assistant camp director caught him one night near camp in an open, compromising position with one of the girls, a camper.

After the scandal had blown over, the question as to what to do with Mark came up, and it was in this discussion that the director was able to get the young man to admit that he really was in trouble. But, as with many people, with Mark too, recognizing a problem and doing something about it were two very different things.

Sitting in the office of the camp director, averting the man's eyes and overwhelmed by guilt, Mark agreed that he had no inner control over his impulses, did things he regretted afterwards, was confused, and needed professional help.

Of course, he had to leave camp and return home, where he was to see the man with whom the camp director had made an appointment for him.

Mark's father listened to his son's explanations for having lost his job, and saw no objections to Mark's seeing a psychiatrist. Perhaps it was a good idea for somebody specially trained to talk to Mark, although privately and in his discussions with his wife, Mr. Metcalf thought the whole idea of "treatment" a bit exaggerated and overdone. In many ways, the father, who had married very young and had hardly known girls, liked the idea of his son's having many different experiences with the other sex before he settled down. The only thing the father considered a problem was Mark's lack of tact or discretion in his dealings with young ladies. That this required a doctor of the mind seemed far out, in his opinion, but he also admitted that these days everything seemed to have to be done scientifically and by experts. He was willing to pay for a visit to a doctor, and hoped that this would clear up Mark's troubles.

In the meantime, Mark went back to his old job, where he was welcomed with open arms, and worked as well as before, got a raise, and started to save his money. He had not asked his parents about it, but for a few months now he had found himself preoccupied with a shiny, powerful motorcycle, the kind that one of the boys in school had been driving for the past year. Mark had been admiring the kick starter, the elegant muffler that produced the tremendous roar, the handlebars that you only had to turn with a flick of the wrist to fly down the road, getting up to eighty, ninety miles an hour in seconds. He even had tried on Bert's white crash helmet and his high boots, agreeing with the mirror that he looked terrific.

His mother was the first one to object to the outfit and the whole idea, which seemed to be in contrast to Mark's conservative tastes, but his father took the usual neutral position, declaring that if Mark wanted to pay for this, it was "up to you."

The issue became central when the psychiatrist, whom Mark had seen two times, proposed two sessions weekly, a new idea for Mark and his family. Everybody had thought of seeing the doctor in the same way one sees the family physician, for an occasional checkup or for a few visits during an infection; nobody had ever heard of seeing a doctor for a year or two, week after week.

Not only was Mark utterly unable to consider such a proposition —"After all," he said, "I'm not crazy, you know"—but his father, too, was appalled at such a plan. Aside from all other objections, he declared his financial inability to pay for such a long, ongoing expense. If Mark were to contribute as best he could to his own treatment, the doctor told Mr. Metcalf, he would be putting something of himself into the experience. The young man was twenty years old, and should take some financial responsibility, particularly since his father was not able to carry the whole burden. Mr. Metcalf liked the idea of Mark's helping with the expense of his treatment, but doubted that his son would be ready to spend his money for something he did not believe in very strongly.

Mark was candid in his talk with his parents. He liked the doctor, he said, a friendly enough guy who seemed to try his best to understand his patients. Personally, he could not see that he had to go on and on, talking about girls and stuff, and he certainly would never, in a million years, spend his money for paying the man. Going there had not been his idea in the first place, but that of the camp director, and to some degree, Mother.

Mrs. Metcalf emphatically agreed. She wanted Mark to continue; if necessary, she would go back to work for it, if money were the problem, but neither Mark nor Mr. Metcalf would hear of that. "I'd feel like a heel," Mark said, "if you went back to work for me, while I'm spending my money for a motorcycle. I couldn't accept it." "Then pay for it yourself," Mother demanded, "instead of wasting your money on this stupid thing that can only cause more trouble."

Mark left the room in a huff, feeling very much misunderstood and hurt. How did Mother dare call the one thing he dreamed of a dangerous menace. He had the model all picked out, looked every day into the show window, and had given his down payment the day before. In fact, as he told Bert, he cared more for his Harley-Davidson than for any girl he had ever met. He was crazy about that baby, could not wait to ride her and roar down the freeway on a clear night, when no cop would bother him.

There was little talk about continuing with the therapist, and no definite ending, but rather a gradual fading out of a very brief experience which had not meant much to Mark, except to establish the fact that he had problems which could cause him further and more lasting trouble.

Curiously enough, this knowledge did not lead to reflection and meditation or anxiety, but was woven into the tapestry of his self-image, producing a more alluring and interesting Mark. When he would drive to parties on the outskirts of town, or to the beach, and girls would hang around the handsome motorcycle owner, he would hold them off by announcing that "I am trouble." Countering their laughs and denials, Mark would assure them that even a head-shrinker had told him that he was trouble, and that any girl with sense in her pretty head was well off staying away from "Mark, The Make-out Man."

As expected, this only increased his desirability and popularity. While in the past Mark had chased girls and felt a small measure of responsibility when his behavior caused serious problems, he now felt completely free of any guilt over involvements with both girls and fellows. He would tell one and all that they had been warned by him, that he was not to be trusted, that he was no good, irresponsible, trouble, and somebody to stay away from.

With the label of "Mark (Trouble), Make-out Man" as a passport to any wild, unbridled, irrational acting-out, he became the daredevil, anything-goes hell-raiser who was ready for any stunt or orgy that he could ignite with the right mixture of inflammable personalities. Nothing was too way-out, nothing mattered. Drinking provided the spark that set off the conflagration, given the proper setting, such as a deserted beach house owned by the parents of one of his satellites, where furniture was smashed, lamps used as targets for pitching practice, boats used for fantastic sexual displays by a whole group. There was the shrieking of overstimulated girls, accompanied by the scream of rock 'n' roll records; there were the way-out jazz boys with electric guitars and loudspeakers turned to top volume; there were the drug specialists, youngsters who got high on LSD, mescaline, pot—Mark right in the middle and always feeling protected by the knowledge that he was "trouble."

Side by side with this weekend behavior went another Mark— the young man who held his part-time job and was charming and friendly; Mark, the student, who barely avoided being kicked out of school for too many cuts; Mark, the young man from a nice family who took the garbage out and bought his sister an expensive cashmere sweater for her birthday from his own money.

When reality caught up with him, when the owners of the vandalized beach house hauled Mark and his friends into court, together with their parents, it was Mark's mother who cracked under the strain. Feeling responsible for her son's behavior, feeling utterly ineffective and useless, Mrs. Metcalf broke down and had to be hospitalized for what was called—"a nervous breakdown."

Mark's reaction to this was an overpowering urge to get away, as far as possible and into a situation where his behavior was definitely limited and prescribed. When Bert and two of his pals, who had not gone to college, were volunteering for the Air Force to avoid the regular draft, which was to reach them within a short time, Mark joined them and applied to the Air Force, hoping for the kind of setting in which he would be more protected from his inner troubles than he had previously been.

His father had no objections, expressing the common idea that the Army, or any branch of the service, would "make a man out of him," and even his mother, from her hospital bed, welcomed this step as the only solution they could envision to the problem of helping their handsome and troubled boy.

# 5

# Walt White

## *"The Crazy Kid"*

Until he had been held up for lunch money by the head monitor, Walt had refused to believe all the nasty stories he had heard. The idea of being forced, *forced* at the point of a knife, to turn over his lunch money to a bigger boy sounded corny to him, ridiculous, something out of the movies! He was, in fact, a tall, lanky young man himself who did not look like the victim of a gang holdup. But, of course, his appearance was deceptive. Walt was anything but a fighter; on the contrary, he considered himself a coward because he had refused for over a year to carry a knife or fool with homemade guns. He would grin, his big homely grin, when other kids told him that you had to carry a knife in Harlem.

Walt always grinned because he was an oddball, and he knew it. He wasn't called the "Crazy Kid" for nothing. The things he liked to do were so crazy that he didn't dare tell any of his friends about them because they would have started such a ruckus with their howling laughter that some fool would have thought it was a riot and called the cops. Walt White not only liked to read poems; he even wrote poetry himself. And, as if this were not funny enough, he also had taught himself to play the piano at the old upright in his grandmother's parlor. But what really got him into trouble was his talent for drawing. This was one thing he hadn't been able to keep secret, because his fingers just naturally found a pencil and a piece of napkin or tablecloth, and before you knew it, Walt had scribbled some lines on it, lines that all of a sudden turned out to be somebody's face. He never really planned it that way; he just doodled, but you just knew that in a few minutes this doodle would turn out to be one of the kids in class, or the assistant principal, or maybe some famous face like Louis Armstrong, or President Johnson, or some gorgeous girl.

Drawing these gorgeous girls had started it. Somebody had discovered that White could make pictures of girls, and the word spread through Abraham Lincoln High so rapidly that Walt couldn't keep up with the orders that poured in. First, it was just any girl, then, girls in bathing suits, next, girls with almost nothing on, and then, girls and boys making out. The funny thing was how Walt knew what these things looked like, since he himself had never even kissed a girl. But somehow he knew, and his drawings were considered hot items on the market. Not that anybody ever paid Walt for his artwork. They just kept bothering him or pestering him or threatening him, until he came up with the genuine article. It was true that the girls looked like the ones in "True Comics" or "Babes With Whips," but nobody particularly cared where White got his ideas from—as long as he produced.

When a teacher, who got hold of one of his drawings, asked Walt whether he knew what "pornography" meant, Walt grinned and shook his head. But that they were dirty and should not be done was clear to Walt. He thoroughly agreed with his teacher that these were not particularly nice, that in fact he preferred to go to the museum on Saturday mornings and copy Rembrandts, but stopping these drawings turned out to be a problem. It seems that one of the monitors, who was quite an operator in his own way, had cornered the market on Walt's drawings, and sold them for a quarter, or even fifty cents, completely unknown to Walt. It was this monitor who made it clear to Walt that he had to go on producing if he wanted the protection he had had in school all along.

Protection was one of the items that were sold for a price at Abraham Lincoln High, and this Walt knew from a hundred stories. You could buy protection against the late-room monitor, against the cafeteria monitor, against almost any gang in or around school. Ordinarily, if you came late, you had to go to the late room where the late-room monitor was to put your name on the list that would be sent to the assistant principal. Nobody wanted his name on that list because the assistant principal, after three late marks, would call in your parents or, even worse, give your name to the truant officer. And this was almost as bad as having a police record. The only way to stay away from this list—if you had to be late—was to pay off the late-room monitor. He charged fifty cents for the first time and a quarter thereafter. Sleeping late could become expensive, particularly if you had only a dollar-a-week allowance.

Until Walt had become squeamish about his drawings, the monitors had taken his artwork in lieu of cash, but now Walt too had to produce money, like every other boy. It took him a while to recognize the stark reality of his school, but ignoring it, or telling his mother about it was no help. Mrs. White, who ran the little grocery store (while her husband tended furnaces for several private houses), became so alarmed that she got somebody to take care of the store for one morning and went to see the principal of Abraham Lincoln. Dr. Saunders was very nice and polite, and assured her that in his school the monitors were the best-behaved and -disciplined boys, so that stories about holdup and blackmail were wild exaggerations of her talented, but somewhat imaginative son. There had been excesses on very rare occasions, but the monitors, though they belonged to their own club—which should not be called a gang—were of great help to the administration because they helped to keep discipline in a very large and difficult school. Would Mrs. White please disabuse herself of the notion that Walt was a victim of the underworld!

When she told Walt what the principal said, the young man listened in silence for a long time, took off his glasses, and wiped them dry. He had not meant to cry like a baby, but the idea of not being believed was truly distressing. To whom could he go now with his torn-up, conflicting feelings? Where would he get the money to pay the monitors if he refused to continue making dirty pictures? He did not like to fight; he never had handled a knife, and the whole idea of violence made him sick. Where was the way out?

Something must be wrong with him that he was so unable to fit in anyplace. Maybe he was crazy or sick in the head or something. Nothing was right. When the English teacher read *Hamlet* out loud, Walt wanted to listen, and kicked the guy next to him who insisted that he pass a note across the aisle. History was interesting, just to think of the fascinating connections between politics in the

French Revolution and the fighting that came from it—you could understand what was going on right now a lot better this way—but he was too embarrassed to admit such ideas to most of the other fellows in his class, because history was square.

His father would tell him to do what he thought was right, and never mind what the other boys were thinking. If he were ever going to be anything, he would have to learn to be true to himself, regardless of what the others thought.

His mother's advice was more applicable: "Shut your mouth; don't talk unless you have to; mind your own business and work hard; say your prayers and remember what you have learned in Sunday school."

It worked for some things, but not for others. When the teacher asked a question and kids giggled, should you raise your hand because you know the answers? If you did this too often, you were teacher's pet, a wise guy, or a rat who queered everybody.

And after six kids have copied your homework, should you admit to the teacher that your work had been the original, or should you make believe that you too had copied it? If you told the truth, the others were in trouble, and you would get it from them. If you lied, you were in trouble with the teacher for copying, and would get it from him. You were in trouble either way. In fact, Walt discovered, you were in trouble all the time, no matter what you did.

There was no way to be popular, or even just get along. Maybe he should never have stopped his drawings, because the gang had left him alone as long as he had produced. Now, kids jumped him in the hall, demanding his lunch money, the jackknives glistening, and Walt went without food rather than fighting or telling on anybody. There was no use anyhow, because who would believe him?

One of the older boys talked Walt into buying a knife, and gave him lessons in how to use it, how to push the button so that the switchblade jumped out, and where to stab, but Walt was so inept and jittery that even his protector lost faith in him. Walt was a loser from way back, and trying to fix him up was just a waste of time. Walt himself knew it and threw the knife into the Harlem River one Sunday morning after church. He felt better seeing the circles on the water and knowing that this old knife was going down fast.

If they asked him, he would say he had lost it. They would believe him—he had lost other things.

The one thing he had never lost and had protected at all times was the valuable Swiss wristwatch that his grandmother had given him when he was sixteen. It had belonged to his grandfather, who had worked on the railroad—in the yard, never on the trains—a grand old man whom Walt had known when he was very small. After Grandfather's accident and death, Walt had gotten this watch, which was his link to the past and a great treasure. He never understood afterward what had made him wear it to school one day, but he had done it and had landed in the hospital as a result of this mistake. The big boy who had spied it and demanded it, when Walt had emptied his pockets and proved that he had no money, had not planned to hurt him that badly, but as he told Walt, he shouldn't have put up such a fuss over an old potato. Walt had kicked and screamed and lashed out like a crazy kid, even when blood was running down his legs and messing up the clean stone floor in the hall.

Walt's grandmother was the one who stepped into his life decisively, after the hospital episode, and demanded that his parents take Walt out of this jungle of a school and put him into a private school. She went further than that. She gave Walt's parents the name of a private school—a name she had gotten from the people she worked for—and did not rest until Walt's father and mother had gone down to see the principal of the private school. Nobody had put much stock in the old woman's ideas, but to Walt's amazement, his parents came to the hospital, just before he was to go home, to tell him that they had gotten a scholarship for him, a full scholarship, provided that he could pass the tests the school insisted on giving.

The thing that nobody could understand was Walt's seemingly strange behavior after he was notified that he had passed the tests and been accepted in the school. Instead of being glad to be out of the clutches of the monitors, as his grandmother put it, Walt was afraid he might be too late in starting someplace else, with mostly white kids who had funny ideas, and in a neighborhood that was as foreign to him as a distant country. At least, in his old school he knew everybody, and many kids knew him. He had made some name for himself as an artist and a screwball, but he was no stranger to his community. They laughed at him, ridiculed him, or pitied him; some even considered him with awe—calling him a mad genius—but he had been on familiar ground.

Now, in the new school, where he was the only Negro boy in an all-white class, Walt felt lost. The class was small, you had the same four teachers, you didn't pay for your food, and in the cafeteria, teachers sat down with students sometimes, talked about discrimination, politics, birth control—very strange topics with which Walt was completely unfamiliar.

What was most bewildering and incomprehensible was the fact that everybody was interested in him, and tried to do things for him. Walt told his parents that he felt on parade, everybody looking at him and being so nice that he couldn't understand it.

Everything was different. In the old school, you had to wear a white shirt and a tie every day. In this one, you could wear anything. No two boys wore the same thing. In the old school, you had to read from page fifteen to page thirty. In the new, you got a long list of books and you could choose when you read them, and once you had finished reading, there was no quiz, but a discussion about this book and related ones. Learning was different. Eating was different. Dressing was different. The kids were different. Walt was not really very happy in the nice new school, and secretly wished he could go back to where he came from, monitors, gangs, and all.

On the other side, there were compensations. The art teacher had become a friend of his in a very short time, and the music teacher had offered to give him piano lessons once a week after school in the empty auditorium. She was young and pretty, and Walt liked it when she touched his hand with hers to correct his finger position. Although everybody called teachers by their first names in this school, Walt was very hesitant to call her Vera, as all the other students did. He persisted in calling her Miss Daniels, no matter how often she suggested he could call her Vera. Walt, who found himself increasingly preoccupied with fantasies about Miss Daniels, and spent hours practicing at his grandmother's old piano, considered her first name too intimate, almost as if she were his girl friend, the ultimate fantasy, reserved for the time before falling asleep.

Whether it was his infatuation with the music teacher, or a preference for music over the other arts, it appeared that both in art class, as well as in his English compositions, Walt, in spite of all the encouragement from his teachers, did not produce anything but good copy-work. When the whole class went to the museum to copy a masterpiece, Walt was outstanding, but when he stood before an empty piece of paper or a blank canvas, he had no ideas and asked teachers and students to give him assignments. He longed for the orders he had received in the old school for prescribed drawings; even if they were dirty, at least he had known what he had to do. His English teacher commented more frequently on his lack of imagination and the stiff, rigid expressions, both in his compositions and in his poems.

Instead of becoming freer in his artwork, he spent whole weekends producing precise imitations of a crumpled pillow, indicating every dent and shadow, hundreds of crinkles and tiny hills, executed with the accuracy of a high-powered lens. To please his English teacher, he memorized poems—a task that came easy to him—but was at a loss when he was asked to write a précis of a story, or comment on a play. To compensate for his lack of ideas, Walt spent every free minute reading, often until late into the night, devouring book after book, trying, without success, to remember what he had read with so much intensity.

When he was not reading, he was practicing the piano. He practiced mostly scales with the metronome, playing with accuracy and increasing speed. Again, he remembered the easy sonatinas and finger exercises very quickly, and got immense enjoyment from his new accomplishments. He played for his parents and his grandmother, invited neighbors and a few children to his house. To everybody's delight, he was able to play any of his pieces with rapid speed and the precision of an electric piano.

Miss Daniels, who had been excited by his rapid progress, was beginning to wonder about his musicality. She gave him different composers, very early Baroque to the Romantics, but Walt played all music alike, whether it were a Bach fugue or a romantic, playful piece by Debussy. He learned to use the pedal correctly, he learned the structure of a sonata, the difference between Beethoven and Brahms, but when visitors came to listen, they had to give him credit for his technique, but also had to admit to his teacher regretfully that this young man had no feeling for music at all and played without any real perception or depth.

Walt was completely unaware of his lack in all the arts, and continued to build in his mind an image of a budding young artist. His family fully supported this fantasy, and everybody was shocked when one music school after another turned him down on admissions tests. Walt was convinced that this refusal had to do with his race, and accepted it as part of the discrimination of which he had heard so much during his school days. While Miss Daniels never supported his ideas, she also did not have the heart to tell him the real reasons for his having been refused admission in the good music schools.

Walt suggested that since his trouble with music had to do with his being a Negro, he should take advantage of this fact and, instead of playing classical music, specialize in jazz and improvisations. Miss Daniels saw no reason to discourage him, since she had become convinced that music was never going to be more than a pleasant hobby for him, and as such, jazz was as good a diversion as any other music. She went as far as to help him find a jazz pianist, who took him for a high fee and taught him the chord progressions and basic aspects of improvisation.

To Walt's disappointment, playing the piano without music was next to impossible. It was like the empty canvas, or the blank piece of paper on which he was to write a poem. If he had to make things up all by himself, he was lost.

In the meantime, he had continued with his studies and graduated with his classmates from the little private school, feeling good about the degree, but also feeling isolated as much as he had throughout his two years at the school. Most of the kids in his class had applied and gotten into college, while Walt was still hoping to make his way as a musician or an artist.

In addition, his family counted on him to help in the store for part of every day, particularly since his mother's heart trouble had become worse during the last year. She needed Walt to lift heavy cartons, bring supplies up from the basement, carry boxes from the delivery truck into the little storeroom.

She had never insisted that Walt stay home, and even encouraged him to apply for colleges on a grant, but by the last marking period, he was just about an average student, in spite of all his hard work. Except for one small college way out west, no school offered him a free-tuition scholarship. Walt himself refused the college in the West because he had figured out that he would never have the money to come home for vacations or holidays, and would again feel left out. Staying close to home seemed safer.

It was safer, but it was also very lonesome. Occasionally, he met some people from the old school, but he usually hurried away from them because he had never gotten over feeling guilty for having deserted his old gang for the fancy white private school downtown. He grinned when the old cronies asked him what he was doing, and told them that he was very busy practicing the piano and making pictures and running his parents' store. The kids listened to him, shook their heads, and walked away shrugging their shoulders.

In the private school Walt had made one friend, a young girl from a broken home who invited him to visit her at one of her two homes, her father's penthouse or her mother's flat in a walk-up. Walt was not very comfortable in either of these homes, but went occasionally to escape loneliness. Sometimes he went to visit Miss Daniels, who always greeted him affectionately and acted as though he were still a child prodigy, a gesture that set him up for days.

Most of the time, he sat in the back of the store drawing details of packing boxes or reading, having decided that he should know as much of Shakespeare by heart as he could. Customers who came for a bottle of Coke or a quart of milk wondered why Walt always appeared as if he were sleepwalking when he came to the front of the store, but were satisfied with his explanation that he had been studying.

Although he had lost interest in playing the piano, he continued because his grandmother had, at great sacrifice, bought a new upright for her grandchild, and he could not let the old woman down. She was happy to see him come in once or twice a week and get to work at the new Krakauer Piano.

When he began failing to hear customers calling from the front of the store, when he had become so absorbed in either his drawings or his memorizing Shakespeare, his mother became worried. Gently, but firmly, she interfered with his obsessional reading by sending him on more errands and trying to encourage him to work out at the local YMCA. While Walt became a member and went for a swim once a week, he remained completely isolated, never making contact with any of the other young men.

To please his mother, he curtailed his reading during the day and sat up the better part of the night reading and trying to remember what his eyes had seen on the pages of his many books. He had noticed that his head had begun to hurt when he was not reading, and that this occupation had become an addiction. At the same time, his eyes began to hurt, a complaint that was not helped with even stronger glasses. The tiredness came only in part from not having gotten enough sleep. It continued even after his parents insisted that he turn out the lights by midnight. To ease the pain, he developed the habit of pressing his hands against his temples, looking down at the book, or if he had no book, to the floor.

The head pain and the tired stages interfered more and more with his daily life. He did not get orders from customers straight and made serious mistakes with the cash register. When his distressed mother pointed out to him, on repeated occasions, that he had given change for a ten-dollar bill, while he had received only a one-dollar bill, Walt grinned and told her that he was sorry, but, clearly, his regret carried no weight. It was without any genuine feeling.

There was no more contact with the young woman from the private school, no contact with boys from his old school or the Y, and, except for the rare visit to his grandmother, Walt had withdrawn from all contacts, and lived in a world of his own. His parents had difficulty talking with him because he seemed to misunderstand anything that was said to him. When he complained of being shunted by everybody, his mother told him that it was he who had isolated himself. He should go out and mingle with people, she said, instead of sitting in the dark back room with his books. She assured him that you can't have both—isolation and popularity. "You can't have your cake and eat it too," she said. To this, Walt replied, after a long reflective pause, "But I don't like cake." At first, his mother thought that Walt was a wise guy who was sassing her, but then she realized by his clouded face and his hands against his temples that he was serious. He did not understand what she had meant.

Again, it was Grandmother who spoke out with determination and insisted that Walt see a doctor. He must be sick in the head. Walt had no objections, and went with his mother to a physician recommended by the people for whom Grandmother worked. The doctor, who gave Walt many tests and sent him to another doctor, who gave him different kinds of tests, called in Walt's parents and told them that there was nothing he could do for their son. The young man had a mental illness which was going to get worse. The doctor predicted that as the head pain increased and Walt withdrew further from all people, he would have to be sent to a state hospital where they had the facilities to treat him. To the question of Walt's recovery, the doctor gave only evasive answers. The parents understood that Walt was a very sick boy who was likely to get worse.

They waited almost a year, during which Walt began talking to imaginary people, and then made the painful arrangements for his institutionalization.

Walt does not mind being where he is, because he is allowed to read to his heart's content, and is not forced to talk to anybody. The medicine seems to ease his dreadful headaches, and aside from his regret over the missed visits to Miss Daniels—to whom he was engaged, as he tells the other patients—Walt has only one objection. He does not like so many crazy people all around him, specially on rainy days when you can't sit out in the garden.

# 6

# Susan Spencer

### *"What's Wrong With Turning On?"*

When her class is dismissed, shortly after three in the afternoon, Susie and her four best friends meet near the drinking fountain across from school and start out on their hunting expeditions. None of the girls need to steal lipstick or kerchiefs, pocketbooks or brief-cases. Their families are not rich, but they are comfortable enough to buy their children the necessities. In fact, the girls don't lift things from the ten-cent-store counters to keep them. On the contrary, they always make it a point to put them back. This is, in fact, part of the game: to take things without being caught and, later, to put them back without being caught.

Susie, who is the natural leader, invented the game and introduced some of her pals into it because it was even more exciting if several girls did it. You would look nice and ladylike, act as normal as possible, buy some things, look around, find out who the store detectives were, and then seek out a quiet corner where no salesgirl was waiting at the moment, choose something—anything, put it in your pocketbook, wait a while to see if somebody came up to you and asked for the money, and slowly walk out with the feeling that you had gotten away with something. It is a pretty exciting game, this seeing how much you can get away with, how much you can get around laws, prohibitions, limits set by society, by the world of adults, by the limits of reality.

The girls would walk out singly, meet, compare notes, show what they had taken, and an hour or two later, or even the next day, return to the store and put the things back again, just to prove to themselves that parents, teachers, counselors, radio, television, and newspapers are all wrong. There was a lot the high and mighty grown-ups didn't know.

Life would have been terribly dull for Susie without her kind of excitement. Like going for a drive in the family car, stopping at every single red light, observing all the speed limits, and never passing when the sign said, "No Passing." What kind of fun was this supposed to be?

Packing one of the boys' hopped-up jalopies with a case of beer, driving with the gas pedal down to the floor on an icy road—there was danger, high adventure, excitement!

Susie has always loved danger. Riding in the ferris wheel, with the safety bars up was so much more exciting than sitting safely back and knowing that nothing could happen. If you know that everything is going to be OK, why start the whole thing? The fun is in taking chances. Lots of chances. The more, the better.

Water-skiing with a life jacket is dull. Diving off the board, after waiting in line, no fun. The wildest boats, the roughest water, the steepest hills for skiing, with as many trees in the way as possible— these are for Susie.

Motorcycles are terrific because you feel as if you're flying and can pass anybody, just anybody. Airplanes are nothing much, but jumping off with a parachute and not opening it until the last minute —there's one of Susie's dreams. She would give anything to be able to do that.

Her mother will tell you that Susie has never known fear, not even when she was very small. She couldn't have been more than two, her mother says, when she just walked out of the Laundromat and explored the neighborhood, while Mother's back was turned for a moment. "I found her on the lap of a big cop in the station house, surrounded by policemen who fed her lollipops and candy! And it didn't get any better when she got older. I tried to put her in a nursery school because I had to work after my husband's accident in the shop, but no nursery would keep her. She would just wander out of the yard and be gone. She just did whatever came into her head. 'No' or spanking didn't mean a thing to her."

Susie has heard about possible dangers all her life—all her seventeen years—but it's gone into one ear and out the other, because it has no meaning to her. She has never experienced any pain from her kind of behavior, and does not really believe that she could get hurt. In some ways she believes that she is protected, or, as one of her friends said to her, "Somebody up there likes you, Susie." Other youngsters who never wore rubbers or raincoats would come down with colds and running noses. Not Susie. Most kids, who filled up on soda pop and ice cream before dinner, would not be able to eat or would get stomach aches. Not Susie. Nothing seems to bother her, and it is understandable that she does not take the warnings of the adult world seriously.

Nothing in life seems terribly serious, nothing very drastic, inevitable, or absolute. There are always alternatives, detours out of tight spots. When the academic course in high school became too demanding, Susie changed to the commercial course, in spite of her teachers' assurance that she could do better, and was bright enough to do well. As long as she liked a subject she did pretty well with it, and those assignments that could be finished in a short time did not cause her any worry. Long-range assignments—term papers or bulky books that took weeks to read—were out of the question for Susie. She just couldn't be bothered. These tasks would have meant thinking things through, worrying about meaning, reflecting, and getting all mixed up. Susie wants none of this. School is a concession as far as she is concerned. Just getting up and appearing in class at a given time—every single day, rain or shine—is almost more than she is able to achieve. As far as she is concerned, she is being very good if she is in her seat before the bell rings, with the most urgent homework for the day done.

The one and only important thing in Susie's life is to keep things casual. That's one reason why most adults can't talk to her. They talk too much, too long, on and on. After a minute or two, Susie tunes out. It's a drag and a bore. The same goes for fellows. They call her a fox, a cute dyno, because she makes out in the back of a car or on the beach, and never gets serious. Once a new boy from a different town asked her for a date, and Susie just looked at him when he asked her if he could kiss her goodnight. She was quite sure that there was something wrong with this character. He just wasn't for real or something; he sounded like her parents or grandparents. As far as she is concerned, somewhere during the night you find a spot somewhere and have a good time, without thinking too much about it, or stupid love talk, or smoochy stuff like that. Sleeping with boys isn't what it's cooked up to be, as far as Susie is concerned. It's pretty exciting, but nothing like getting high when you turn on.

This is one reason why Susie hardly ever goes out with one fellow, but usually stays close to her gang, or looks for parties where she knows there are lots of kids. Turning on by yourself is a drag, doesn't mean a thing. In fact, it just isn't done.

You know the right crowds and you know that somebody will have a nickelbag and if the others smoke pot, you do too, if you're a regular. Turning on is about the only thing that means something to Susie. She could even get serious about that, because when you turn on in the right crowd, you're really living. Everything is twice as sharp and clear, you can hear the singers on the records take a breath, and red isn't some dirty rose or pink, it's honest to goodness loud, brassy RED. You can smell pot and you can touch a guy's hand and there are ten thousand little hills and valleys on the skin, each one making different music, and you're loose, real free, and you really move, everybody moves, the whole joint is jumping, you dance, and you couldn't care less because you feel great!

Other times, turning on does different things to you. Like the one time when Susie and her best friend tried to write their names after they were high and the funniest thing was that their handwriting was like that of an eight-year-old, real funny, large letters and scrawling all over the page up and down. You feel like a little girl and you can laugh like a kid because you are a kid and at the same time you know that you're not a kid at all and can do what any grown-up can do. It's the greatest feeling.

Compared to pot most everything else is pretty dull, to tell the truth. It's all right but you still want to get back on pot. Not that Susie is hooked. She tells anybody who should ask her that she doesn't have to turn on; it's just that she likes to.

Somebody talked addiction to her, and she laughed in his face. "I can stop any day I want to," she said, "and do you see me 'taking a trip' and getting hooked on LSD or opium?"

Susie could of course be classified under one of the many impulse disorders, with the low frustration tolerance and the particular nature of her acting-out. The reader could get a full clinical picture detailing the early traumata and the ways in which the ego failed to develop in several significant areas. One could choose to consider her verbalizations mere intellectualizations, attempts to rationalize and cope with the all-pervading anxiety. It would not, however, give us the fascinating interplay between pertinent criticism of society, the denial of her own inability to face up to any limit of her own inner boundaries, the highly complex mode of her ambivalence, and the many ways in which she is coping with it.

Rather than considering clinical data or interpretations, we may get a richer picture of this young woman if we let her speak for herself. This is life as she saw it until her commitment to the treatment school at Briarcliff.

"Sure, turning on is against the law; that's because we have the wrong laws. Most laws are wrong. Like getting married. Easy as pie, anybody can do it. But try to get out of it once you've found out that it doesn't work. You have to make up a million lies before they split you. Should be the other way around. Make it hard as hell to get married and make it easy to get out of it. Wrong law.

"Getting a driver's license. Any idiot can get one. Nothing to it. But have a drunk bump into you and it's your fault. After you're in trouble the law gets tough. Why don't they make it real tough to get a license, make you pass a hundred thousand tests and stuff, instead of waiting until you're in trouble? Wrong law.

"First couple of years in grade school when you feel like learning, they just fiddle around. Comes thirteen, fourteen, nobody wants to go to school; don't let them kid you, anybody who tells you he likes school is a liar. You have other things on your mind, believe you me. But no, law says you've got to go to school. Wrong law. That's the time to work, use your hands and muscles. By eighteen when you become interested in things, you've got to work and can't learn, unless you're a genius. When you're really ready to study things, when you hear about election and voting and politics and you want to read, you've got to pound a typewriter some place or feed your husband. Wrong again. Everything the adults made is wrong.

"No use talking about it because who listens to a kid, a teenager? I'll tell you who listens to us, the smart guys who make the zoot suits and the jumpers and the Ten-O-Six Lotion by the gallon and the *Guns and Ammo* magazine and the program *Shindig*—the smart businessmen are the ones who pay attention to us because kids spend millions and after you've read *Hot Rod* for a year you want to have one of your own. Big Business listens to us. I know a girl who tells them what we like to eat and wear and she gets paid for it. It's called Market Research. That's who listens to teen-agers. Guys who can milk us. It's a laugh.

"Grown-ups are no different than kids. They're trying to live it up, only we know how and they're too chicken to be different from the guy next door. Grown-ups always come on big and make like they have the answer. And if that isn't a laugh!

"I've asked hundreds of kids I know how many couples they can name who are happy. I mean just getting along. Married people, parents, grown-ups. It's like sex. It's not what they say it is. Like most jobs. You've got to eat and so you stay and it's supposed to be cheaper for two and you stay together. But I haven't met a single couple that was happy. Only in the movies and the old books.

"So, what's wrong with having a good time, with turning on and stuff? We're not hurting anybody and don't tell me we're hurting ourselves. We're OK, we're getting less hurt than most grown-ups with their worries all day long and their being jumpy and getting mad at each other and screaming at the little kids. My mother runs to the doctor all the time and the medicine chest in the bathroom looks like a drugstore and my dad sleeps. He sleeps all the time. He comes home from work and eats and reads the paper and before you know it he's asleep, or else he falls asleep on the barcalounger watching TV. That's what we're supposed to copy?

"I'm sorry for my kid brother and my little baby sister. They're supposed to shut up in the morning because Dad is still sleeping and after dinner they're supposed to shut up because Dad is tired. If they play, it's the wrong game. Too much noise. Don't make a racket. If they want to turn on a program, my old lady says it's not for kids. They'll be delinquents if they watch that sex stuff. So the kids yell and Dad comes out and whams them one and they scream some more and I do the dishes and get the hell out as soon as I can.

"What else is there? Staying around the house is the biggest drag ever, even if everybody is gone. TV puts you to sleep with their crap about murder and this crook and that crook and bodies floating in the water and stuff. Maybe things like this happen to one person in a million but I know oodles of kids and they know mil- lions of kids and nobody, but not a single one, has ever had any- thing to do with murder and smuggling and creeps like this. Why should I care who killed who? And that gooey stuff could kill you even worse. You don't talk about things like this, for pete's sake! It's like meeting somebody for the first time and you start to bawl because you feel lousy. That's private, love is or what you call it, sex or stuff. I think it's embarrassing to have to watch two people kissing. That's their funeral. Why do I have to watch them. If I like to make out with a guy I just do it, but not with some camera guy around. Imagine kissing for a camera! Just picture that.

"That's another thing adults don't know anything about—pri- vacy. Not that damn drawer in your room or that silly bit about a corner where you can make out. I mean real privacy, like I told that headshrinker who wanted me to go to some creepy place with other kids like myself and get straightened out. Imagine living in a place with five hundred nuts like myself and everybody creeps along the hall and sneaks into the office where the headshrinker sits with a white coat. When you come out the other kids want to know, what you talk about, what he say? It's embarrassing, man, I wouldn't want everybody to know that I'm crazy and see some headshrinker. That's my business, not that I would ever see a creep like that but if I did I sure wouldn't let anybody know. It's like going on the john on the street, in broad daylight. Some things are private and I don't care what anybody says.

"Like what marks you got or how old you are or religion. What's the big difference what you think when you make up something in your head, that's your business, isn't it?! Nobody can prove it to you. So if somebody wants to think that there is somebody with a long white beard sitting up in the cloud, let him. What harm is he doing? I mean it's all private anyway, what you call God or Country and stuff. The Flag! What that? A piece of cloth, different sizes and somebody sews on these red and blue stripes—union wages—and then somebody carries it around on a stick and you're supposed to get all hot and bothered about it and skip a heartbeat! For a piece of cloth! I know, I know about that bit about the 'symbol,' I've heard that one too. Who needs it? I don't need it. My kid brother needs it, he sticks these little flags all over his bike and pedals like mad and pushes that silly horn, scaring everybody on the street to death. It's kid stuff. I don't need it. I know my name and where I live. Yeah, yeah, the history, you're not supposed to forget about that. OK—remember the Boston Tea Party? We had a great time, man, drinking tea and throwing the stuff in the water. I got a B in history, sitting up half the night memorizing the stuff until morning and a good thing too that history was first period, because after lunch I'd forgotten half of it. Who can remember all that nonsense?

"I remember that history test because it was the last one I took in P. S. 47, because when I got home that afternoon—dead tired— there was that man talking to my mother about me. That's how it started and, boy, don't these goons try hard to earn their living, like the cops who've got to come home with a ticket or else no promotion. To this day I don't know who tipped this character off about pot but he got nothing out of me, brother, he could stand on his bald head for all I care. Whoever gave him the idea that I was on LSD I don't know, not that I wouldn't have tried it—I try anything once for kicks—but it so happens that I didn't know anybody who had any. What made me laugh was when he got started on that business of me pushing pot. Me, big operator Susie! That's one for the books. Of course, my old lady was a real pal, I'd say that for her. Not that she came right out and told on me—she doesn't know anything anyway—but did she act like a mother and throw the goon out? I don't know what she told him before I came home but I wouldn't put it past her to rat on me. She would too! Maybe she figured now is her chance to get even with me. Parents can't stand to see you feel good. You're supposed to be serious and worry and stay awake half the night and be 'responsible'—that's her favorite word. It means worry and get jumpy and all jittery. Like her and Dad. He wasn't home that day or maybe he would have thrown the fink down the stairs, but my old lady—oh, boy!

"They hunt you down till they catch you; they can't stand to see you feel good. If not for pot, it's got to be for LSD or for heroin, and if they can't prove that, they say you are a thief and steal from ten-cent stores or you're truant because you've been absent a trillion times or you're a crook because you have copied stuff and tests twenty thousand times. Delinquent. You're a delinquent, boy, and the judge is going to throw the book at you. Jaydee Susie. Your mother tells us that she can't do a thing with you, you're uncontrollable and come home all hours and don't take the dog down every night.

"So OK there was that boy who promised to cooperate with the cops—that goon was from the narcotics squad—and he swears that I'm hooked. He's got it from me, says the liar, but he's the good one, the one who 'cooperates' and me, I'm the bad one. Take your choice.

"A regular courtroom with long seats and a big desk up high and a flag in the corner and this woman in the black outfit. Serious. Gad, are they all serious! I'm not supposed to smile. I'm supposed to cry. I don't feel like crying, is that OK?

"If it hadn't been for my old lady I would have just gone back home and back to school, but she tells the judge she's fed up, can't handle me, I'm too tough for her. Dad has nothing to say as usual, he just stands there and looks scared, poor Dad. How he ever decided to marry that bitch is beyond me. A nice guy, my dad, but he ain't got a chance with her. 'It's up to her,' he tells the judge. 'I'm working all day; she has to have the say about it.'

"In a way I'm glad. It's out in the open. All her talk about worrying about me and taking care of me and sacrifice this and sacrifice that and I'll be the death of her and she's freezing all winter because she bought us kids something to wear—all this baloney about your ever lovin' ma is for the birds and I've always thought so but now I know. It's my own mother who sent me to that place. Her and nobody else. So OK. I'm going. For a year and when I come back I'll be eighteen and I wished I were a boy so I could join the Marines. They should have something like it for girls.

"I'm only sorry for my little sister and maybe my kid brother, but more for the baby because she is going through the same things I went through with the old lady and she's going to be in trouble even before seventeen. I can tell because I know her.

"The old lady didn't even come to see me at this shelter where they keep you locked up for a couple of weeks until they ship you off to the reform school. A creepy place this shelter, like a jail only they make believe it's a fancy boarding school. They have bars on the windows so you don't jump out or run away and inside they have these tables with checkers and these old women with oodles of keys who come around and act like you are a sick cat. Once in a while you have to talk to some doctor or social worker. They really give me the creeps. If they would ask you questions, like a cop or the judge at the court, but they don't do that, they want you to talk—so they just sit there and wait for you. You are supposed to tell them what's on your mind. That's what the doctor says to me, 'What's on your mind, Susie?' If that's the way headshrinkers act they have another guess coming. I have never even met the guy. He looks OK but I don't know him from Adam and he expects me to talk to him as if I am an old pal of his. Makes no sense to me. And if you ask him a question, they don't answer. They just sit there and look you over like you were some guinea pig and then he writes something down about you.

"I ask him, Why do I have to come here? He tells me to work out my problems.

"Damn if I know what he's talking about. I ask the other girls but they don't know any more than I do. So I go and talk to the man, why not, it's better than sit around and play checkers or read *Ivanhoe* or *David Copperfield* or the intelligent funnies, the ones with the message. The food is lousy and at night some creepy girls have nightmares and on Monday you get clean sheets. If you're athletic, which I'm not, you can play volleyball with the boys. One of the boys I know, he has connections and promised me half a nickelbag.

"This same guy is being shipped to Briarcliff, the same 'college' I'm going to be in. He's a sharp operator, wants me to put out if I want the stuff. OK by me. He's a nice enough guy, as long as he keeps getting the pot once in a while. Specially out in that joint with all the floosies and prostitutes I've heard about. I'll need something to keep me going. You can't get through a whole year locked up in some place, a hundred miles from civilization, with a couple of headshrinkers and social workers and making out with some guy. I hear they have school there too, for morons; you read Little Red Riding Hood in twelfth grade. So this guy is going to be my friend, for this year for sure . . ."

# PART II

# Some Causes

~

# 7

# Obstacles to Understanding

Our six young people are in trouble, each in his or her own way, but all evoking in us feelings of compassion, sorrow, or anger. One cannot help but ask about causes of their difficulties and wish that there had been somebody along their paths who could have understood and helped. Not only understood, but understood deeply enough, for "understanding" is used both for surface observations as well as for the depths of clinical uncovering of early and long-forgotten developments.

Whether we understand on the manifest level or through deep analysis, we are subject to "blind spots," as Freud reminded all of us, professionals and laymen alike. The responsible clinician tries to become aware of his blind spots, his "resistances" to understanding, through his own personal analysis, in which he attempts to bring the hidden, unacceptable feelings of his own past to the surface of conscious, reachable knowledge. Parents and leaders, educators and clergy—all people who want to understand and help but usually cannot avail themselves of this safeguard, can nevertheless go a long way toward recognizing many of those feelings that tend to interfere with objectivity.

While each parent or teacher has his own individual resistances and obstacles toward understanding, there are some common interferences that we can examine in this chapter.

## Our Guilt May Interfere

Probably one of the most prevalent obstacles to understanding is the common myth of the forever-concerned parent or teacher. This myth underlies much of our writing and talking about young people and their troubles. It suggests that most adults have practically nothing else on their minds than to understand children, adolescents, or young adults. One almost gets the impression that adults have solved most of their own problems and can now use their time and energy and compassion to be deeply concerned about youth. We know that every one of us has his own very complex life, with a great many unresolved conflicts, yet the myth persists, because of the burden of guilt on the part of many of us who have something to do with youth.

Of course, there is genuine concern and devotion—but not nearly as much as some of us would like to believe. It would be more accurate to say that people feel that they should be deeply concerned, that they should always be available, that they should stand by and be calm and reasonable. It is the same "should," the same superego, that makes us pay taxes, go to the voting booth, keep a disagreeable appointment. But while we can go to the voting booth or fill out our tax returns with this feeling of obligation, it will not help at all when it comes to understanding young people.

For young people sense very accurately that we are concerned—not so much with understanding them, but with having them act the way *we* think they should.

If they don't, we ask, "What did I do wrong?" implying that we are responsible for everything that happens inside the mind of the young person. This is a kind of omnipotence, masking as responsibility. Our own guilt leads to overindulgence or rejection—but never to understanding.

When the guilt gets overwhelming, we project it on the young people and make them omnipotent: "It's all your fault"—my migraine, Dad's ulcers, and our quarrels. The young person will defend himself and tell us where to get off—which makes us furious —or he will buy our projected guilt and feel overwhelmed with remorse, making us wonder what happened to make him act so meek and mild.

It is not difficult to see how we fell into the role of the all-knowing, all-powerful authority. Certainly, during the formative years the child needs to feel that the parent knows all, controls the world, his world. The child's dependency and faith are very gratifying, and although we have no need for it intellectually, we do come to accept the role the child wants us to have.

In adolescence, young people get annoyed at their parents and teachers because these adults fail to live up to the roles into which they cast them when they were growing children. The adults' response is to try to recapture the gratifications that come from being admired and respected. We redouble our efforts, only to be rebuffed by the rapidly expanding minds of the young people. Our last-ditch stand is our economic superiority; we have had more practice than the young people in earning a living and providing some kind of financial security.

When respect is gone, when reason no longer has any appeal, we frequently use our last resort—we refuse to pay, or we say sarcastically, "Pay for this nonsense yourself," knowing very well that this is the one thing young people are prevented from doing by the structure of our economy. Youth is kept out of the labor market by the intricate system of arbitrary demands that are placed like hurdles along their path, forcing them to delay their development until they have graduated with what is known as the union card, even though their bachelor's degrees in no way equip them for the beginning jobs which they now may take, at minimum wages. They are bewildered, they are angry at being held back from doing what they want to do, and if they cannot do what their elders are doing economically, they can try their hand at other pursuits which they have seen adults engage in: they can drink, they can have sexual intercourse, they can protest—until we get so threatened that we call the police and lock the rebels up. "Be quiet and read your books," we say; "play at self-government and enjoy your financial dependence; make all the noise you want, experiment and grow a beard; just don't mess with our adult society which we have tried to build up for some forty years. Pretty soon we shall retire, and then you can take over and see how good you are at building a better world."

The recognition of our own hostilities, of our very mixed emotions about young people, enables us to be just a little more objective and to separate our needs from those of our youth. This is not a punitive, counter-hostile attitude. On the contrary, it is an honest admission of our limitation. We are usually ashamed to admit that we don't want to understand certain behavior. We usually say, "I can't understand it," implying that we would like to comprehend it. This is not always the way we really feel. Sometimes we should come right out and say that we really don't care that much, if we don't. A frank admission, even if it is a negative one, is a sign of respect for youth and for ourselves. Understanding takes a great deal of libido, care, patience, time—all of which we have to some extent. But it is not unlimited. Why do we pretend that we are so very eager to be of help and want to do everything possible?

Young people complain forever that their parents or teachers don't really listen, don't pay that much attention, and remember nothing they have been told. It is quite true that many of us are not in the emotional condition to listen as intensively, over as prolonged a period of time as young people may like. Why do we pretend? It would help if we gave a concentrated quiet hour, and made it clear that this is our limit. We are not helping if we forever act as if we had endless patience and interest.

We ask for an honest response from youth. Let's be very candid ourselves about our own interest and our limitations.

### Some Obstacles

If we don't face these limitations in ourselves, we will fall back on a number of responses that are not helpful. All these responses derive from our own guilt and hostility, and while they will relieve our own anxieties, they make things more difficult for young people. Many of us may not be ready to undertake the tough job of really understanding troubled behavior, but we are also not interested in doing harm to youth. For this reason, it may be useful to list a few of the responses derived from our own problems that are either not helpful to young people or, at the very least, act as obstacles to any kind of useful communication.

## Scapegoating

A fairly characteristic obstacle is *scapegoating,* that ancient symbol of discharging evil. In our day it takes the form of questions: Why did you do this? Who is responsible for that? Whose fault? You recall the way Mr. Tibbett blamed the college for Tom's behavior. Certainly somebody must be at fault, and if we can point the finger, we certainly feel a lot better. Originally, according to biblical law (Leviticus 16:10), the scapegoat was a goat upon whose head were symbolically placed the sins of the people, after which he was suffered to escape into the wilderness. These days it does not need to be a little billy goat. It can be New York City or Chicago, the company he keeps, or the school he is in, the magazines he reads, or the television programs he watches. It can, in brief, be anything. And just as the ancient sacrifice of goats has not affected evil in the slightest, our scapegoating will not help us to understand a thing; on the contrary, it will alienate us even further from the already distant young people.

If, for instance, we talked to Susan Spencer, and were interested in learning about her use of marihuana, it would not help in the least to ask her, "Who got you into this awful mess?" or, *"Why* are you doing this?" but it might be useful to ask her, *"How* did you first get interested in pot?" This question would lead to a discussion of the process in a fairly objective and non-judgmental way, which would be necessary if we wanted a young woman like Susan to talk to us at all.

## Cliché Thinking

If we reacted to Mark Metcalf by saying, "Oh sure, I know the type; these fast kids are all like that," we would not get one step closer to understanding the cause of Mark's behavior. We would not even be close to any comparable group of young people, because the concept "fast kids" is a cliché.

It has been recognized, even in the clinical field, where one works with individuals or small groups, that diagnostic labels, though valid, may not be meaningful enough and may typically act as an interference to a more meaningful understanding. The general use of such diagnostic concepts as "neurosis" or "schizophrenia" or "borderline states" is diminishing, as thoughtful workers have come to recognize that to call, for example, Walt White "schizophrenic" would not tell us very much about him, except that some aspects of his personality are not in close enough contact with reality, or that he is suffering from some thinking disorders. A rich, detailed description of behavior is always preferable to a diagnostic label or category shortcut.

Some categories seem to be specific at first glance, but on closer observation turn out to be so broad as to obscure meaning and better understanding. To talk of "neurotics" is as meaningless as to talk about "juvenile delinquents." There are millions of "neurotics," and the category tells us nothing about Linda Lewis or Tom Tibbett.

Another concept that is often cliché thinking is "environment." The concept is used for two very different purposes: (1) to denote the early relationship of the infant to the mother and (2) to denote the social, economic, cultural environment. One describes the psychological conditions, the other the sociological factors. When these two different meanings are used interchangeably, the concept "environment" loses its meaning and becomes a cliché.

Take Gwen Grant, for an example. She comes from a lower-middle-class, rural New England background; she was reared in a definite social climate—of which we have more to say in a later chapter—she was educated in the county school and went to the Catholic Church in the town nearest her home. Her father's income, the shortage of work in the county, the politics of the selectmen, the Army Engineers' flood control project, which brought employment and money for some small luxuries—these and many other important factors could be classified under sociological conditions.

All of them would help us to understand Gwen Grant as one of the many young people reared on the old county road. None of them would help us to understand Gwen, as distinguished from her two sisters, her friends, her contemporaries. One of Gwen's sisters

is now teaching French in a large high school, planning to continue her education and get her Ph.D. in French. Gwen's brother,
the one individual to whom she could relate, is comfortably well
off, has a large, relaxed family, is a man full of self-confidence and
humor.

You could not explain Gwen's "I don't count" attitude, nor her
sister's social mobility and drive, merely by the sociological factors
in their background. To understand Gwen as an individual, you
would need to look at the psychological "environment," the early
relationship of Mrs. Grant to her last-born girl, the way in which
the mother's unconscious and conscious attitudes facilitated or re-
tarded the small child's growth in the formative years.

We would have to study the basic "environment": the mother-
child separation, the relationship to siblings, the ordinal position in
the family, the father-daughter relationship, the interaction between
sisters and parents, and the enormously complex dynamics of over-
lapping currents of drives and expressions, between all members of
this intricate unit, the Grant family.

We use a cliché when we say that Gwen's parents were poor and
had no education to speak of. We use another cliché when we say
that she went to a church with an aging priest, in a community
where her religion was in the minority. We are using clichés all
along if we try to throw light on the particular character of Gwen
by referring to sociological factors, since these same factors apply
to all young people from the same community. The point is that
psychologically nobody has the same environment. The environment, the constellation of the family is different for the first and the
second child, and each of the young people who went to mass in the
same town had their own individual perceptions of the common experience, just as a class of ten art students would produce ten
different paintings of the same model.

On the other hand, we would be guilty of a psychological cliché,
if we talked about Walt White and ignored the fact that he grew up
in a community where many young people of his age felt they had
to carry knives. This would not be true for the culture of a Tom
Tibbett or a Linda Lewis. For Walt, this fact is significant, as is his
role as a member of a minority, particularly when he went to the

private school. We would be using a cliché if we talked about Walt's isolationist tendencies as a withdrawal symptom, or if we spoke of his shallow affect separate from the role he played in his culture.

While it is quite true that we can find this kind of affect in any environment, Walt's particular personality, growing in a community that necessitated further withdrawal on his part, facilitated the gradual break with reality. We could not explain his peculiar gifts, his naïveté and fears, primarily by the turbulent environment in which he grew, although we might consider the possibility of Walt's growing up in the quiet county road of Gwen Grant's home, where he might not have had to worry about protection and real dangers in the outside.

The culture can facilitate or prevent healthy growth so that, on balance, neither the psychological environment nor the sociological environment, taken separately, is sufficient to help us understand young people. We need to understand how the basic character structure develops in the first five years, so that we have to concentrate first on the intra-personal and intra-familial conflicts, before we study the external conflicts in the neighborhood, community, and the world outside.

To use "environment" in the cliché sense, the nonspecific, general sense, cannot help us to understand young people. This use instead becomes another obstacle.

### Over-Identification

This obstacle is difficult to detect because it is covered up with a layer of reasonable, sensible outward behavior, while a few inches below this image, there is a secret, just barely concealed pride in the daredevil, unconventional, bizarre behavior of some young people. One can detect this note of secret pride and projected omnipotence in parents when one hears talk about the young person's disturbances and serious pathology, together with an assurance about his "brilliance," his "highly original mind," his "fantastic gifts."

It would be absurd to say that Mrs. Spencer liked the idea of Susan's smoking marihuana. Of course, Mrs. Spencer thought this was just the worst thing a young woman could do—of course, she did everything in her power to stop Susan—but to some very good friends, she would admit that she could think of worse things, that this could be considered another crazy, passing phase of behavior. Susie was not smoking it very often, and from what the mother had learned, it is not habit-forming. Susie was just impossible, really, always up to something, new ideas, flying all the time, coming up with the most fascinating ideas, crazy perhaps, but at least she was not a dullard. You would have to admit, Mrs. Spencer would say, that Susie is a very "interesting" young woman.

It is subtle and not fully conscious, but Susan has caught the secret admiration all her life and has always known that her mother did not really, deep down, mean No when she said No. The over-identification comes across in the way Mother would look at her, or in the tone of her voice, rather than in the words. Put in another way, Susan has not had the real, firm boundary against the desire to act out every impulse. Mother's No was not for real, and sensitive young people know the difference very early.

This over-identification not only deprives youngsters of developing a better inner control, but it also prevents parents or leaders from really understanding what is going on. The issue after all is not that Susan smokes pot or plays at stealing, but how this behavior developed, and what made it necessary. The over-identification prevents us from a more objective view of the total personality. Susan was, after all, suffering from depressions and had suicidal tendencies, which are far more significant than any given symptom, no matter how undesirable socially.

Or take Mark Metcalf, whose father definitely over-identified with his "charming" son. In his case, over-identification takes the form of seeming confidence: "Anything Mark does is OK with me." He gives his troubled son carte blanche, which paves the way to least resistance. It prevents the young man from making solid contact with reality, first by unwittingly encouraging him to act out his early, undeveloped instinctual drives, and after the acting-out, which seems to have no consequences in his life, he is prevented from recognizing that he has real problems.

Mr. Metcalf has to believe—as do many fathers—that since he

is supporting his family, is not drinking or having extramarital affairs, and is contributing to charity, he is the so-called "normal" person who has no problems himself. It follows then that any son of his, too, must be another "normal" individual, equally sound and reasonable, "right as rain." Mr. Metcalf, in fact, said, "We have given him sound values, and we expect him to live by them."

With the assumption that all is well with Mark—because he is "my son"—Mr. Metcalf has repeated the favorite American Illusion of Self-Reliance, the self-made man, the above-average, forward-looking Liberal, no run-of-the-mill dullard; in fact, "The Metcalfs are different." Whatever difficulties Mark or his sister may have, Dad can straighten out, and besides, time will take care of such passing problems, a Metcalf can help himself, and furthermore, you should not worry or get too introspective. "I have," Mr. Metcalf has said over and over again, "one hundred per cent confidence in you."

As with Susan's mother, Mr. Metcalf secretly admires his good-looking son. He considers Mark's behavior as a sign of virility or "masculinity," believing that he has ample proof that Mark is not suffering from homosexual problems, which indeed underlie his compensatory behavior. Believing that his own difficulties with girls throughout his youth were the result of his economic difficulties, which forced him to concentrate on earning a living, Father is reassured that at least his son is making up for the good times "the old man missed."

## Carte Blanche

Mark, with his father's carte blanche in his pocket, behaves as if he were wearing an amulet, a magical protective device, so that he never needs to be concerned about his behavior, no matter what he is doing. This, and his natural charm, will always get him by and keep him out of trouble.

Father's over-identification has made it almost impossible for Mark to consider his own problems and certainly has prevented Mr. Metcalf from understanding what is really bothering his son.

If over-identification is used as a technique of leadership, or as a device in counseling, education, or therapy, it will also interfere with understanding; it may lead to further alienation between leader and youth, or it may produce dangerous acting-out.

A more harmless example would be the young sociologist who proposed to "understand" members of a hostile gang by merging with them, by joining their activities, after which he planned to exert his influence on the young people. He dressed as they did, talked as they talked, and became one of the boys. He considered this a form of acceptance, and for a time went along with the gang on expeditions and antisocial behavior. He learned a great deal about holding up stores and techniques of street fighting, and wrote up his experiences in a book. The youngsters who encountered no interference from their "leader" admired his role playing, kidded him along, and felt a little sorry for this well-meaning adult who was trying so hard. They did not ever trust him for a moment, realizing that this man was not of their culture or background, and could never have their values.

The youngsters went on with their gang behavior, and the young sociologist went back to finish his degree, feeling that he had learned a valuable lesson: that understanding or cooperating did not mean over-identification or merging.

Since the healthy parts of the ego are usually operating and re-jecting the irresponsible or acting-out behavior, it must follow that young people cannot respect any adult who tries to help them by condoning their actions, tacitly or otherwise.

Neither Susan and Mark nor the young members of the gang, respected their parents or leaders whose over-identification had worked as an obstacle to understanding.

*In Brief:*

Because many of us don't care as much about young people and their problems as we would like, or as we believe we should, we suffer from feelings of guilt which, in turn, lead to attitudes and actions that interfere with an objective, clear understanding of young adults. Our own behavior may relieve some of our anxieties, but it may also act as an obstacle to comprehending the behavior of young people.

Some of these obstacles are scapegoating; a tendency to categorize or to label, either in plain language or lingo, by the use of clichés, popular, sociological, or psychological; by over-identifying with young people or giving them carte blanche.

# 8

# The Young Adult (I)

A greater awareness of our own blind spots will help us to see better, but it will not tell us what to look for. What is significant—the long hair, the beards, and the jive talk, or the ideas hidden behind the folk-rock? The protest songs or the motivations for them? Is this just a modern version of the familiar phenomenon—one generation superseding another, the rebellion of the young, the *Sturm und Drang?* Or is it really something very different?

From all indications the answer seems to be—both. We will have to look for the psychological characteristics of this particular period, post-adolescence. We will also have to try to look for the particular sociological and cultural characteristics of young adults in the United States in the mid-sixties. This chapter and the one following were conceived to treat these aspects of the problem.

As was suggested in the introduction to this book, the period between the late teens and the early twenties has not been sufficiently considered. The following pages represent an attempt to state some of these characteristics of the post-adolescent period, as distinguished from the adolescent and the adult images. Where it is appropriate, reference is made to related writing in the literature; these references are keyed to the Notes at the end of the book.

## The End of Role Playing

There seems to be agreement among psychoanalytic investigators of adolescence that role confusion or diffusion exists at this phase of development. While this is undoubtedly a pertinent aspect of the adolescent ego, one is more impressed by the realization on the part of young people that time is running out, that role playing will have to terminate shortly, that long-range and binding choices and decisions will have to be made. It seems that this threat, in the face of the incomplete integration of the total personality, represents a source of anxiety and accounts for some of the behavior of the six young adults with whom we are particularly concerned.

In order to appreciate fully this impending threat, we should reconsider briefly how adolescent role playing came about.

During the basic "normal disturbances"[1] that characterize adolescence proper, role playing is a necessary substitute for several incompletely developed functions. The adolescent will seize an activity that he can handle and which gets him by. He will play a role that protects him from being too uncomfortable: he may be "The Strong, Silent Type," he may be "cool," he may be "Show me, I'm skeptical," he may be "The Brilliant Young Man," she may be "The Gal Who Can't Be Shocked." Tom Tibbett's role for a time was "The Socially Dedicated, Earnest, Bright Man of the Campus." Mark Metcalf's role was for a time "The Well-Dressed, Casual Make-out Man."

These roles can be changed, the way make-believe roles are changed in latency, when one can be a policeman one day, a gangster the next, or earlier, when one plays cops and robbers and can change roles within moments. Earlier, these games included, besides changes in occupations, also changes in sex: in playing house, one may be the mother or the father, the baby or the big sister. Role-playing games are one way to try to master reality and cope with internal conflicts.[2]

The role playing of adolescence is usually accompanied by changes in appearance, tastes, language, mannerisms. It often also brings changes in affiliations, opinions—particularly social and political, embracing of causes, or becoming involved in a great variety of organizations. All of it represents attempts at adaptation to the adult society.

The adolescent's role playing is by way of experimenting both with powerful internal conflicts[3] and with powerful external reality pressures and demands. In spite of the seeming intensity of the nature of role playing, the expressed belief that "I mean it!," and the apparent determination to carry out each role as a permanent function, the adolescent does know—if he is enabled to express his conflicts and doubts freely—that this is not the end of role playing. He knows that he can always change his mind, that nothing drastic will happen if he does. He can still sleep in his bed and be assured of three meals a day and enough pocket money for fun. If he changes his mind and gives up that job, or flunks out, nobody will evict him, haul him into court, or take away his meal ticket. He is still "underage." Role playing still has aspects of play.

Susan Spencer, whose attitudes were somewhat premature for her phase of specific development, expressed well the post-adolescent anxiety about the threat of the impending termination of role playing when she said about College Boards and Regents' examinations: "I'm not worried because my Boards may not be over five hundred; what worries me is the *finality* of all these tests."

The cognition, or the recognition—and the difference between them may be significant—that there is a limit, that choices will have to be made, is often a severe threat to the young adult; his infantile omnipotence—that the sky is the limit, that you can be anything, do what you want, go anywhere in the world, and always be protected and safe—still lingers. As Linda Lewis put it: "I haven't made up my mind yet if I want to be a true lesbian or go straight."

This entire anxiety, heightened by the realization that role playing is coming to an end, is accompanied by the increasing necessity to present—at least to others—a fairly consistent picture of one's self, even though one may not have come to terms with what this image is like, or should be like.

## The Self-Image Dilemma

This second characteristic of post-adolescence may be illustrated by a typical episode in the life of Tom Tibbett, one of the six young people.

After having studied late one night, Tom woke up very early the next morning because his civil rights group had planned a protest march through the downtown section of the town, where many restaurants had refused to serve Negroes. The sky was gray, it was raining, and Tom was still very tired. He half admitted to himself that he would rather stay in bed and sleep a few more hours, particularly since he had a final examination that afternoon and a date at night.

For about fifteen minutes Tom struggled actively with the disturbing dilemma. Why should I get up and be tired for the rest of the day? . . . Do I have to go to the protest march? . . . Sleeping would do me more good and help my examination. . . . The girl won't be sympathetic to my tiredness at night since she doesn't believe in protest marches. . . . But is it not my responsibility as a socially conscious citizen to participate in the civil rights struggle? . . . Am I just looking for an excuse to sleep a little longer? . . . I'd better get up now and stop stalling around—but isn't the examination real and important?!

The whole drama lasted but a few moments but it serves to show what goes on a great deal of the time in the mind of the young adult whose "self-image" is assailed on one side by the demands of his strict, often rigid conscience—his "superego"—and on the other by the idealized picture of himself, the part that is called the "ego-ideal." What the young adult hopes to attain is a stable, balanced self-image, a reliable view of himself which remains more or less steady throughout life. In trying to reach this representative self he is torn by the values of his family, his community, conflicting groups among his contemporaries. Does he align himself with the right-thinking people although he does not like the way they behave —or with the very friendly people whose opinions he does not accept?

What indeed is the self-image for Tom at this moment of crisis? Is the wish to sleep longer really just an excuse for his "laziness"? Is it realistic to rest before an examination? Or is the examination a minute issue compared to the civil rights battle that affects millions of citizens and is part of history? The ego-ideal, the freedom-loving, patriotic Great Democrat, the follower of Lincoln and Paine demands that Tom—like every man—do right by his President and his government: Rise and protest injustice! The self-image, of a studious, serious scholar who believes that anything worth doing is worth doing well demands that he come rested and relaxed to a final examination. And his strict, somewhat punitive superego pushes from the other side: Are you "copping out"? Are you a quitter, an irresponsible character who should be looked down on by his contemporaries?

The self-image dilemma is very real. It means being pushed by several sides, and we have not even considered the numerous permutations possible in this dilemma. We only have to mention the voice of Tom's mother as compared to that of his father, his adviser as contrasted to his favorite professor, his date of that evening and the view of the other girl he would rather have gone out with and his many close friends, who all have their own self-image dilemmas.

A few years earlier, at the height of adolescence, it was still possible to live with one's self-image by doing the expected thing or by doing the opposite. One could live with oneself by doing things *because of* parents or the establishment, or *in spite of* authority, home, school, community.

A few years hence, in the late twenties or early thirties one usually has succeeded in resolving this dilemma to some degree.

Most of us have reached a fairly consistent compromise within ourselves, a compromise arrived at by trial and error, determined by the friends we were able to make and keep, by the partner we finally settled down to live with, the social and political currents in which we had to learn to navigate once we had chosen a career and moved in a definite direction. Except for rare moments or certain auspicious occasions, we are as used to our self-image as we are to our reflection in the mirror.

In the hiatus between adolescence and adulthood, however, the self-image dilemma is constant. The internal forces are constantly churning and burning up energies.

What the healthy young adult often does to cope with this dilemma is what most of us do when we are in conflict: he gives in to that part of his personality which is the most demanding, whether he likes it at the moment or not. Tom Tibbett got up that morning at six and went on the march, cursing himself every step along the rainy way.

The self-image dilemma was more serious and led to longer-lasting complications in the case of Linda Lewis, as in all situations of young adulthood where the different aspects of the personality are so far apart from each other that the ego cannot succeed in effecting a workable compromise, a balance in living.

Linda sees herself as a talented, but constantly exploited human being, as somebody who never had any luck and was unwanted from the start. She would consider her detached, "cool" behavior as a necessary part of her self-image, as the only way in which she can cope with a harsh and unyielding world.

Next to this self-representation we can discern an entirely different image of herself, her ego-ideal, according to which she would have coped with the role of the exploited "beautiful" female and been a man instead (a role she acted out in her lesbian relationship), a completely self-sufficient, brilliant artist who would be above demands of reality and requests by authority.

And if the self-image and the ego-ideal are worlds apart, her superego, based on the demands of a demanding, punitive mother, nearly tears the self-image to pieces and gives the young woman not a moment's peace. This harsh superego demands that she be a conventional wife, a well-groomed young woman with middle-class standards who is intelligent, but not too sparklingly bright, who is industrious, but not unduly zealous.

Without attempting a clinical, analytic description of Linda, we can well understand how this young woman was engulfed by her self-image dilemma, and had no way of coping with it except by bizarre, unrealistic behavior and, finally, isolation.

For still another example of a very different self-image dilemma, we may take Gwen Grant. All along, her self-image had been that of an ineffectual, unsuccessful girl who couldn't do anything well. Her ego-ideal was in sharp contrast to this self-image: the picture of an extremely self-reliant, independent young woman. It had become almost a defiant struggle against the meek, downtrodden self-image with which she had lived so long. It was this ego-ideal which, in a way, had led her to take on the almost too demanding challenge of a marriage to a widower with a child, as if she had embraced the ego-ideal with a vengeance and clung to it fervently.

Once she had begun to take on the new role, her superego, related to the ego-ideal, had become an interference in her relation to her stepchild. It prevented her from allowing the child to develop her own autonomy, to experience life by herself. Gwen needed to do everything for her, as though this were what she felt she should do, as though she owed this to her self-esteem. Not to do this would have thrown her back to the poor, older self-image and made her feel that she was an ineffective mother.

The dilemma of the self-image was not entirely resolved for Gwen because it had not given her a comfortable basis of functioning in her new role. That the child resented not being allowed to experiment and to do things for herself made Gwen feel inadequate as a mother, but to allow the little girl the freedom to take responsibilities and make her own mistakes would have thrown Gwen back to the self-image which neither she nor her husband could accept.

There is in her life a continuous struggle among the various forms of self-representation, a battle which makes her constantly tired and discontented. We have not at all attempted to show the husband's inner conflicts, but we can picture how the internal forces within each of the three people constituting a family unit must create a continuous and never-ending source of smaller and larger areas of friction. These are not unusual, once we start to take a close look into the complexity of the self-image dilemma of three people who live closely together in one small home.

Whether the superego is too demanding or is inflating the ego-ideal, whether the self-image is too grandiose or too much based on earlier pictures from phases of childhood, during the phase of post-adolescence there is an active battle among the three parts of the personality, a constant interaction among them, leaving the young adult with a persistent and sometimes unresolved self-image dilemma.

## The Struggle for an Identity

This third characteristic of the young adult is closely related to the previously discussed self-image dilemma, but it is not the same. While in the self-image dilemma we notice a struggle among the three different concepts of the self, the struggle for an identity is more a struggle against getting lost and feeling like a stranger to oneself, almost as though one does not know who he is. We may define it as a temporary feeling of depersonalization which occurs frequently and sometimes over long periods of time in young adulthood.

Susan Spencer expressed this feeling when she asked, "Am I really there?" or when she in a poem (see Chapter 13) said, "Help her," meaning, "Help me." Susan was not under the influence of drugs when she felt that she could hear her own voice, listening to herself, watching herself move. For her the sensation of wanting to "get away from myself," the wish to "shed my skin like a snake," the notion that the body and the mind are not all one, but consist of separate, unconnected parts—all were everyday feelings. One day, when the adviser talked to her in his office and asked, "How do you feel about this?" Susan had the impulse to turn around and look behind her because she did not really know to whom the man was speaking, since she did not feel that she was there. She had no trouble recognizing the adviser, other people, objects outside of her self, but she had at times great difficulty recognizing Susan Spencer.

Susan and many other young people sometimes get very concerned about this feeling of alienation from the self, thinking that they are losing control or going "crazy." It would help to reassure young adults that degrees of depersonalization occur in everybody for briefer or longer periods, and are not at all unusual during post-adolescence. If young adults can learn to bear this painful state and live through it, they will lose most of the anxiety associated with this struggle and in time emerge with a more defined feeling of their own selves.

When Mark Metcalf considered enlisting in the Air Force, he talked with friends about the possible experiences or adventures ahead of him. He said, "When you get captured, you only give your name, rank, and serial number. I think that's cool." Later he explained what he liked about this order. "If you know your name, rank, and serial number, at least you are damn sure who you are. Without it, you can't be sure."

He expressed the struggle for an identity in his way. To him "identification" was the same as identity and if we had asked him about it he would have pointed out that people always ask you to identify yourself, when you want to cash a check or want anything from strangers. "I identify myself by showing my driver's license," Mark says. "That's my identification."

Unwittingly, Mark here points to the significant linguistic connection between identity, identical, and identification. Much of psychoanalytic literature is concerned with the roots of identity, ever since Freud emphasized the infantile roots of the ego and particularly since later research verified these early findings in the study of "the first year of life."[4]

The dictionary definitions of "identity" first list the "sameness" as in "identical" before they mention "unity and persistence of personality." It helps in our understanding of this third characteristic of post-adolescence to remember that "identity" originally has to do with "sameness," both etymologically and psychologically. We know now that in the beginning the ego of the infant is not yet differentiated from the ego of the mother. They remain the same, identical for a few months, before any differentiation occurs. At first, the infant's survival and security demand that he identify with the first being outside himself, the mother or mothering figure. He has, at first, no choice but to remain in a state of symbiosis, to remain identical with the breast, the source of nurture. In the beginning of life, identity has to be identification with somebody, with a person outside the self.

As the ego develops,[5] after the individual becomes aware of his separateness—which is only possible under certain conditions of mothering—identity gradually replaces identification. As the ego unfolds—provided it has the favorable environment—the individual discovers his self: my hands, my feet, my toys, my house. With the awareness of the self comes the recognition of other people, that is to say, the social aspect of reality, so that eventually, identity can be defined to include the awareness of the social reality. The term "identity" can then be defined as "a social function of the ego which results, in adolescence, in a relative psychosocial equilibrium essential to the tasks of young adulthood."[6]

What happens in young adulthood is usually a distinct change from the familiar, known social reality to an unfamiliar, unknown environment. This may be starting a new job, entering college and living in a dormitory, being drafted into the Army. The identity which the individual has been achieving is not very solidly grounded in social reality, partially because of his economic dependence on his family, partially because he is still ambivalent about leaving the familiar.

Awakening in a strange room, with strange people; being called upon to perform tasks regularly; the necessity to do what you are told, not what you feel like—all come with the changing social reality of the young adult. He cannot return to the familiar; he is not quite ready to move on. His identity is threatened, and he frequently regresses to identification, as we all do when we are threatened by new, unknown experiences. We search out the familiar face at a party of strangers, we stick close to familiar experiences in a threatening situation—and the young adult is no different. He may react to new, somewhat threatening, and certainly unknown life situations by identifying with some people he can feel "at home" with, of the same or the opposite sex. He may join groups and identify with them, to postpone the identity crisis.

If Walt White had joined the group of monitors in his school, if he had defended them vehemently, identified with them for protection, we would have an example of identifying with a group to postpone the identity crisis. Walt's self-image, his goals as a young artist or as a young man in a turbulent community, would not have been represented by the strong men in his school.

Tom, on the other hand, came to the student council and the protest movement because he had discovered that necessary changes in the society in which he would live could not be brought about by himself, but through social action. He looked for people who thought as he did, and joined hands with them. In the sense in which identity may be defined as a "persisting quality of the experience of sameness,"[7] Tom's participation in the civil rights struggle was one of the ways in which he resolved the identity crisis characteristic of young adulthood.

## The Cognition of Time Continuity

Of all the concepts with which the young adult now has to make firm contact, the cognition of the passing of time is the most difficult. That life is a continuous process has, until now, been merely an interesting, abstract notion. Much of his behavior was still determined by the pleasure principle, the acting-out of instant gratification—regardless of consequences, of effects, of continuity. The differences between his wishes, needs, demands, and what is possible in reality seem to become sharp and clear only now, as he leaves adolescence.

Increasingly, he finds himself hemmed in by objective reality, having to give up what is desirable at the moment, and acting on what is necessary and possible. When the original omnipotent fantasies extend into reality, he is brought up short now, not by the edict of outside authority, but by the cognition of reality and time continuity. The "I don't care" luxury is less and less possible, because the young adult is discovering, with some pain, that the price is too high.

Until this phase of development, it was still possible to act out some of the infantile demands. If instincts pushed the adolescent ego for gratification, as they characteristically do, there was not too much of a price to be paid for acting-out. The moment could be fantasied to represent all that matters, and the idea of next month, or five years from now, had not much more meaning in adolescence than it did in latency. It had only the abstract "I know" meaning. With the coming of post-adolescence, this mode of living is less and less possible. His actions affect not only himself, but others as well, and decisions can no longer be reversed as quickly and painlessly as before.

Time, as a new dimension and measure of reality, sharply impinges on the young adult, as he is asked to make long-range decisions, and finds himself involved in long-range responsibilities which he never had bargained for. This is true for personal relationships, professional or vocational choices, alignment with social, ideological, or political groups.

The idea of planning, the idea of future, the idea of saving, considering details with awareness of their long-range effect and value —these are all new demands on the young adult which characterize this phase of development. Once it was easy to decide what "you want to be." As one young adult said, "You could be anything you wanted—fireman, cop, doctor, lawyer, Indian chief. Now it's for real, and you get scared because so much depends on your decision: what school you pick, what you write down as your major, what courses you select . . . you tell your friends, your family . . . as if you mean it . . . and you can't believe for a long time that you are a bio-major . . . it doesn't mean anything to say that . . . except that this is really what you are . . . your courses prove it, your adviser talks to you as a bio-major, and you are classified as one . . . it's for real this time . . ."

There is, in this young man's statement, the end of role playing, the self-image dilemma, the struggle for identity, and also the coping with time as a measure of objective reality.

While, until this point, the individual had made progressive contact with time throughout the developmental process (learning to tell time, being on time for school, organizing one's work in the time available), it is only now that the continuity of time, as a measure of reality, becomes meaningful. With the move into young adulthood, the individual determines the use of time as an extension of his own identity into the future. He may have learned that the plane does not wait for him, but, as Mark Metcalf discovered, a moment of instinctual acting-out—like sleeping with a girl he wanted—may have consequences extending not only over the next nine months, but, as with Tom Tibbett, over the rest of his life.

Throughout latency and even into adolescence, the method of punishment has obscured the realistic law that actions have consequences. Punishment obscures this fact because it makes it appear as though the consequence is not the result of a natural law, but instead, the result of the parent's or the authority's mean temperament. Only as the adolescent moves into young adulthood and becomes his own authority, does he learn that if he signs his name to a lease, he can no longer move out any time he would like.

He has heard all through adolescence about "responsibility," and cannot stand to hear the word one more time. But it is not until post-adolescence that he experiences the concept, not as an imposed nuisance or demand from the outside, but as the natural result of his action, or lack of action, the response (responsibility) to a stimulus. What has kept the concept somewhat vague and unreal has been his omnipotent fantasies, his early mode of life, based on the discharge of wants or needs, regardless of the effect on the outside world, regardless of how these needs or wants were met.

He has heard about money, sometimes from earliest childhood on, but certainly in the last years of high school, and he has handled money with increasing awareness. That it represents accumulated energy expenditure, a time aggregate, transferred into money only if it meets the needs of somebody else becomes real only at this phase of development, when thirty-five hours of work are required to secure a roof over one's head for one month. Clothes, shoes, bare necessities, which he had gotten as though they came from a never-ceasing spring, now take on a completely new meaning.

In post-adolescence, as the teen-ager moves into young adulthood, the money he spends comes increasingly from his own earnings and goes increasingly for necessities. This is a difficult and not always successful changeover which needs to be taken into consideration as one of the characteristics of the young adult.

## Escape Into Marriage

If adolescence is characterized by sex without love—and love without sex—post-adolescence is more typically defined by escape into marriage. Not infrequently, the young adult, beset by the recognition of an end to the role-playing period, by the self-image dilemma, by the painful struggle for identity, and by the recognition of reality dimensions, makes a quick dash into the approved, established, high-status institution of marriage.

Although he knows that about a fourth of these marriages do not work, he assures himself and others that this is different for him. Since at this phase of development, the intellect is highly developed, it is used to explain away all the real conflicts and doubts described in this chapter. As one young adult put it to his counseling clergyman: "I know all about the problems, but we get along 'intellectually, emotionally, culturally, sexually.'" As the adviser said, an unbeatable argument, foolproof and solid so it seemed, until it was time to work together on the new venture they had created—their relationship.

The very idea that marriage consists of a partnership that requires continuous and everlasting work, care, tact, and patience seems to some young adults quite preposterous. Each of the two partners had barely enough energy to work on his or her own problems, let alone a major third one—the new establishment, the union of a man and a woman, an institution which exists aside from each of the members.

It is not very difficult to understand how many of these marriages fail: they were undertaken in a state of semi-madness, while they were "crazy," crazy about each other, but still "crazy" or "madly" in love, which is a very good definition of the state of having "fallen" into love. The ego, which should be functioning at its best when it comes to making long-range commitments, is barely operating at all, while the instinctual forces dominate the field.

But it is not so much intensive desire for each other or the demand by society to have a license that gets some young adults to undertake a responsibility which they often cannot possibly carry. It is rather an attempt to bypass the characteristic problems of this phase of growth with what seems to be one grand gesture.

To illustrate this point, we may take the characteristics of post-adolescence and observe how they are bypassed in the pseudo-solution called "marriage."

1. The threat to the *end of role playing* is seemingly avoided by yet another role—Playing House. This is particularly obvious when one or both parents of the young couple continue their financial support, leaving the young people in about the same state economically in which they were during adolescence and before. With this arrangement, the reality of time—time for work, for learning, for having fun together—is avoided.

The economic dependency—which also makes the sense of ownership illusory—also increases the hostility between the two generations, which in turn has an effect on the relationship between the young people, because of the deep and complex early involvements either has had with their family in Playing House. The very last of the role-playing experiments is often tragic because it involves another person and sometimes a new generation, a baby which has come into being out of this post-adolescent role-playing extension.

2. *The self-image dilemma* is bypassed by the escape into marriage through creating a seemingly new category—Husband and Wife. This is best seen by the change of name for the young woman. She is no longer Gwen Grant; she is Mrs. Foster—a new name, a new identity, almost somebody else. It is almost like saying: "I no

longer have the dilemma with my self-image, the demands of my superego, and the ego-ideal."

3. And to extend this one step further into the next characteristic of post-adolescence, it is like saying: "I no longer need to *struggle for an identity*. I am practically somebody else"—a husband, a wife, a father, a mother. "No longer need I re-experience states of depersonalization, or not knowing who I am, because I can always get a restatement for my identity doubts through knowing that there is somebody else, that I am no longer alone or isolated. By being a part of somebody else, I can feel myself." If both members of the team have this feeling of identity-substitution, we get the young couple who seem like a house of cards, two babes in the woods, leaning on each other for support which neither has to give. The first strong wind of hostility will have to blow this little house down.

4. The full *cognition of time continuity* is partially avoided by the "rehearsal for life" quality which is inherent in many of the post-adolescent marriages. This is due not only to the partial financial support from the same parental source which shields the young adult from experiencing reality as objectively as necessary, but also to the accrued sense of accomplishment which is not quite realistic. As one young woman put it: "It is not really so different from what we've had before we were married. I still go to my classes and stay on line in the cafeteria, and the same for Bill. When we didn't have to study evenings, we used to be either at my place or his; now we are in one room and have less privacy in a way, if you feel like being alone or reading while the other wants to play a record. Nothing is so very different, really . . ."

Like many other young adults, she too was not sure that the process of marrying was worth it, although she admits that there are some advantages. In the main, however, she takes comfort from the idea that things will be different in a few years, when both can have more control over their time, their income, their planning. Other young people recognize that they did not know the partner until they had lived together, and if one or both had discovered that getting along was more work than it seemed worth, they attempt to dissolve the union—"Call it a rehearsal," as one couple put it.

This characteristic of post-adolescence then—"escape into marriage"—is often an attempt to bypass the many difficult adjustments which make being a young adult a special situation, and often a trying one.

There are other characteristics of post-adolescence besides the five that we have discussed, such as well-reasoned rationalizations of hostile dependency relationships, vigorous struggles against occasional states of depersonalization, but these do not show up as often as the ones listed, nor are they as well-defined.

When we say that the five characteristics are seen in a large number of young people, we should understand that all these five characteristics do not occur in most young people. Some young people may be particularly troubled by the identity conflict, but have no difficulty coping with the end of role playing or the self-image dilemma. Other young adults will be bothered by the cognition of time continuity only, while they may have worked out their identity conflicts.

It is only when all characteristics seem to accumulate in one young person that we speak of real trouble, in the sense of symptom formation and lack of adequate functioning, or failure in adaptation. If we take another look at the six young people from Part I, we will find that each of them showed most of the characteristics of post-adolescence, in addition to their individual symptoms. In other words, these young people got into trouble because their egos had not been in good enough shape to cope with the many normal adaptations that are required at this phase of development. Things had become too much for them, and something inside their psyches had to give. Most of them had enough healthy ego aspects to function in some areas, but we think of them as youth in trouble when, on balance, they experience more pain than pleasure. Emotionally, they are each in the red, their psychic mechanism not balanced out.

### In Brief:

Between adolescence and adulthood we can distinguish another developmental phase of growth: post-adolescence. Several characteristics of this phase have been described and illustrated in this chapter:

1. The End of Role Playing
2. The Self-Image Dilemma
3. The Struggle for an Identity
4. The Cognition of Time Continuity
5. Escape Into Marriage

99                                              The Young Adult (I)

1. The End of Role Playing
2. The Self-Image Dilemma
3. The Struggle for an Identity
4. The Destruction of Time Continuity
5. Escape Into Marriage

# 9

# The Young Adult (II)

Some readers may have reservations about the preceding chapter. They might feel: This is all very interesting—the identity struggle, the end of role playing, and the other internal psychological developments—but what about the times in which the young adults grew up, the social and political climate which surely had an effect on their character formation and should be considered as one of the causes of behavior?

The question is the basic one of "nature versus nurture," the individual and his society, the relative significance of "environment" to the formation of character. This issue has not really been settled satisfactorily by anybody, mainly because it is very difficult to trace the deepest causes of attitudes and to measure with any kind of scientific rigor the effect of one event on many people, particularly young people.

## How Much Did Society Influence Them?

Certainly there are some social factors that clearly have a definite and formative influence on young people. Equally clearly, some very significant political events may have no impact at all on a ten-year-old, or even on an adolescent.

Take, for an example of the formative influence of social factors, the early childhood of people born in Germany during the early thirties. It was understood that they had to join the Hitler Youth and were sworn to loyalty to their organization, instead of to their families, schools, and churches. While this edict would have had individual effects on each member of the Hitler Youth, we would have to understand the structure of the organization, the political and social climate of fascism, to get perspective on young people of this period.

## The "Crucial Decade"

The first half of the period in which our young adults—Tom Tibbett, Gwen Grant, and the others—grew up has been called the "Crucial Decade" by one historian. With a few brush strokes, he recalled some of the flavor of the decade following 1945, which he called a "crazy-quilt era":

That taut Thursday when Franklin Roosevelt died, the first sickening fall of an atomic bomb, the heartfelt roar when Jackie Robinson trotted out in a Dodgers uniform, the meat you couldn't buy and the apartment you couldn't rent, high prices and still more boom, a brilliant young man named Alger Hiss, President Harry Truman now fumbling, now making the bold decision to go into Korea. Arnold Toynbee and Mickey Spillane, Enzio Pinza singing "Some Enchanted Evening" . . . "We like Ike" and chlorophyl chewing gum, Senator McCarthy intoning: "Point of order, point of order, Mr. Chairman," President Dwight Eisenhower worrying millions and reassuring still other millions by his folksy, middle-roadism—these and a thousand other memories flood back from the frightening, heartening, whirligig years after the end of World War II.[1]

Tom Tibbett was born on V-J Day. Perhaps this was one reason why his family could not be out singing and dancing in the streets as families were all over the country. His older brother, who waited with his father outside the maternity hospital, remembers how somebody gave him a little tin trumpet, the kind one usually has on New Year's Eve.

Gwen Grant's older sister dated a fellow who was one of the four million Americans studying on the GI Bill, a young man whose family had always lived near the Grants' farm.

Walt White remembers how his parents talked about the indignities Jackie Robinson had to suffer—that he was the Dodgers' first baseman, but was not admitted to hotels when the whole team was on the road. Walt later confused his hero with the singer Paul Robeson, and was beaten up for his insistence that Jackie and

Paul were the same man, who could both hit a ball and sing an opera.

Mark Metcalf's family moved in the postwar boom into their new garden home in the suburbs, and with them, hundreds of other families settled down, the open yards in the back a natural playground for Mark and his first girl friends.

None of the young people were directly affected by the portentous developments of the time—not while they were entering kindergarten. Neither Churchill's "Iron Curtain" speech, nor the Taft-Hartley Law—which, in fact, did affect Gwen's father and his union at the time—neither the Truman Doctrine, nor the subsequent Marshall Plan meant anything to the four- and five-year-olds. However, it must be noted that this was also the beginning of the Cold War, which was to eventually have a very direct bearing on their thinking, their education, and their attitudes in post-adolescence.

Mrs. Lewis, Linda's mother, did go out ringing bells for Harry Truman, urging neighbors to defeat Dewey—and Linda was left alone for days, just as she had been when her mother had felt she had to work in the defense plant, five years earlier. To Linda it did not matter for whom her mother campaigned. It mattered that she was not at home where Linda needed her.

The Tibbett household was split on the Alger Hiss issue, with Tom's mother very upset over the outrageous accusations, the way Dr. Binger, the psychiatric expert—an acquaintance of her brother's—had been treated by the prosecution, the scandal of what was the forerunner of a period of red-baiting and witch-hunting. Mr. Tibbett, who did not like Ivy League bright and successful men, refused to side with his wife. He took what he called the popular attitude, that of "containment," by which he meant, "Wait and see," while the term more typically represented Truman's foreign policy in the next four years, in relation to the Russians. Tom listened to his parents arguing with vehemence and intolerance, but then again, he had heard them argue just as vehemently about what kind of car to buy.

## *The Influence of Fear*

No single event—by itself—can be said to have had a decisive effect on the character of the young adult at the time of early childhood and latency. But we all know how sensitively small children react to prolonged states of fear and anxiety in their parents and teachers. The Cold War, which characterized the time of their growth from childhood into young adulthood, was bound to leave a mark in the formation of their attitudes, their social unrest, their intensive search for more stable and permanent values.

Do they remember the first hydrogen bomb, which was ordered when they went to kindergarten? Had they actually heard of the "danger of communism," which was the excuse for certain committees to stalk bookstores for communist writings and to try to burn John Steinbeck's *Grapes of Wrath;* or for textbook boards as they set out to "protect" the schools from communism, shielding the young from any praise of the minimum wage laws along the way? People were beginning to use the word "intellectual" as if it meant some compound of evil, stupidity, and treason.[2]

This was 1949, when Mr. Tibbett hesitated to spank Tom—as he had done until now—because his wife interfered, backed up by misunderstood findings of psychoanalysis, progressive education, and the same indignation with which she had protested their older son's having to crawl under desks for shelter during the war.

Neither Tom nor most of the young people of his generation ever heard of the Senator from Wisconsin, who needed a more successful and rousing issue with which to become more important to his voters. Yet it is probable that most of them were infected with the rapidly spreading climate of fear which emanated when the Senator used "The Danger of Communism" instead of "The St. Lawrence Seaway" or "Another Townsend Pension Plan" to ride to dangerous power in the Senate.

From the attack on the State Department to the censure—during a long four-year period from 1950 to 1954, while the young adults moved into latency and were open to learning, open to moods of home and community, open to tensions in school and church—was the time when the honored right to self-determination, the right for redress of grievances, the right peacefully to assemble and to protest, was dishonored and perverted, to be known as treason and disloyalty.

Tom Tibbett's brother, who had already started college, had, like most of the young people in the early fifties, withdrawn and become afraid to care, to think, to speak out. He was of the "silent generation," which was later of such grave concern to educators,[3] statesmen, and, finally, all of us.

We will never know how much the young people actually experienced, to what degree they caught their parents' fear of being dismissed, their teachers' unsureness of handling controversial material, their parents' friends' reporting of neighbors who had been blackmailed into confessions, to avoid the ruin of reputation and livelihoods. How many read the headlines of character assassinations, of evidence of fear and terror in the population?

They do remember the beginning of the Korean War and the burning of controversial books, because they had started to read and were ten years old by the time the State Department—in fear of McCarthy and his associates—ordered books by Communists and fellow travelers removed or destroyed.

It was President Eisenhower, in his Dartmouth speech on June 14, 1953, who urged: "Don't join the bookburners. Don't be afraid to go into your libraries and read every book as long as any document does not offend our own idea of decency. That should be the only censorship."

Not only Dartmouth students reacted to this speech, not only students in other schools. Their families reacted as did their younger brothers and sisters. The historian records that "McCarthyism was permeating every state and every occupation, sometimes ridiculous, sometimes frightening, sometimes bordering on the incredible."

But if McCarthy had used Hitler's slogan of "danger of Communism," our youngsters did not end up in fascist youth organizations. They sat with their folks in front of their television sets, watching McCarthy call, "Point of order, Mr. Chairman," the one line which was repeated by children on streets and in mock meetings. They heard about watchfulness and the need for vigilance. Visiting speakers and the voices over the airwaves—Edward R. Murrow—told them in very clear tones that they lived in a democracy and that it was their duty to protect the democratic rights for which their forefathers had fought and died.

Not many of the ten-year-olds noticed May 17, 1954, when the Supreme Court declared that no child could be barred from a public school because of his color. This was to be the beginning of the civil rights movement in which these ten-year-olds were to play a prominent part ten years later.

Other significant aspects of the period in which these young adults grew up were the growing prosperity and the concomitant fear of depression—a repeat of the crash of '29; a fear that the Cold War would develop into a shooting war—the toy stores reflected the new missile developments—and the suspicion that without defense contracts from the government, our economy might not hold up. Many of the young people recall frequent moving about, change of communities, of schools, of friends, a readiness to get up and go, a feeling of transiency and the formation of the attitude, "Why get all hot and bothered about the kids around here; who knows how long we're going to stay?"

The very quieting of the international scene had many Americans saying: "Wouldn't a peaceful solution and the cutting down of defense expenditures bring the crash?" as the historians record.[4]

## Changes in the American Family

Subtly, the nature of the American family was changing. Women, many of them mothers, made up one third of the country's working force. Youngsters were more and more on their own; there was less sharing and less communication in the home. The TV dinner was born, more and more families sat around the magic box, and every house had the familiar antenna on the roof, next to the chimney. Violence and murder were everyday TV fare, watched while munching the precooked turkey and sweet potatoes in the compartment trays, and—another major departure—Lucille Ball of *I Love Lucy* was seen all through her pregnancy, with week by week changes.

Youngsters like Tom and Susan, like Mark and Linda, grew up on these television programs and on comic books; their families looked for more chromium on their cars and for instant, push-button solutions to complex problems.

All the while, in spite of slow and controlled inflation, the national income went up; one in nine adults owned stock; in the summer of 1957, when these young people were starting adolescence, the country spent "two and a half billion dollars on summer vacations."[5]

Young people got more allowances, helped less, could get more and more luxuries from their parents, started to live in the illusion that the sky was the limit. Surrealism was rediscovered, while the "Organization Man" was described by William Whyte, Jr. The cult of chance became the rage, astrology magazines sold by the millions, as did the more abstract, the more absurd, the more "modern" in art, literature, music. The same shoddy, superficial trend appeared in the "Dial-a-Prayer" lip service, the *Modern Screen* magazine series in which Jane Russell announced: "I love God. And when you get to know Him, you find He's a Livin' Doll."[6] Billy Graham rolled on with the evangelistic crusade, supported by a budget of $1,300,000 during one year.

Can we really assume that impressionable young people, in their early teens, remained unaffected by these developments, retained the values of their parents' childhood, grew up "just like we did"?

## The Beginning of the Space Age—Nudge to Education

Perhaps, one might say, some of the developments of this decade were only of relative significance to children and young people, who, after all, were not directly affected by the changes in the adult world. There was, however, one major event which very directly did affect the lives of every child and young person for generations to come. Sputnik I was launched by the Russians in October, 1957, as our young people were starting junior high school.

The race for space, for the moon, was on, and with it a new orientation in learning. To many statesmen, makers of public opinion, and writers, it appeared that the United States had been caught napping. They believed the country had to revamp its educational philosophy speedily, to be prepared for some future showdown on the moon. Critics of the school system, long ignored, were now in vogue. After the Russians sent a second Sputnik into space, *Life* magazine ran a series of articles on our crisis in education.

> . . . schools have been overcrowded for years . . . teachers are grossly underpaid . . . young minds of great promise get no encouragement . . . the geniuses of the next decade are even now being allowed to slip back into mediocrity . . . no agreement on what schools should teach . . . a quarter of a century has been wasted with the squabbling over whether to make a child well adjusted or teach him something . . . standards of education are shockingly low . . .[7]

Almost overnight, the emphasis in education shifted from the humanities to the natural sciences. Youngsters gifted in math and physics became the darlings of the educational system; they were wooed by colleges and universities, and handed National Defense Scholarships, while grants to study Greek or Latin, the classics or art, went begging.

The young people now in adolescence witnessed a new technocratic revolution with a steady increase in electric brains, the beginning of automation in industry, the rise of the computer, the accent on "science"—which always meant the natural sciences from Sputnik on out. It was a strange revolution, started by the Russians, and taken over by us, with the young people as the pioneers in this new "Space Age."

## Changes in Mores

At the same time, we witnessed a decided change in morality, in manners, in values. The speed of change in the cultural climate, the haste with which adults tried to retool their thinking and style of living, had their effect on young people as well. Stealing books in college was not uncommon, "cheating in examinations was admitted by 40% or more of a large number of colleges, often with no apology, or a sense of wrongdoing," according to one scientific survey.[8]

The emphasis on quantifiable data, on amassing of knowledge per se, had been exploited by television in the quiz shows, in which many thousands of dollars could be won. That Charles Van Doren, a scholar in the humanities, could be bought by this new trap, and ended up with having to admit fraud, was one of the tragic by-products of this period. He was defended by students and the public in general, a commentary on the particular absence of moral indignation which characterized the middle adolescence of our young people. It was not smart to get indignant about dishonesty, it was not cool to make a fuss about immoral behavior; short of outright major criminal acts, anything was acceptable.

The parents and leaders of the young adults were engaged in building the "Affluent Society," a term coined by John Galbraith, the Harvard professor of economics. He made clear that our values came from a period when we had to worry about widespread poverty. Clearly, what was needed was "not the better-equipped American, but the American who was a better human being, his life enriched by an altered community atmosphere and by greatly improved facilities for education, medical care and recreation," as suggested by Professor Eric Goldman, the author of *The Crucial Decade*.

## Adolescent Reactions

As the adolescents grew into young adulthood and peeked above the fence behind which many of their individual growing concerns had been lived, they saw little on the horizon that was truly challenging or meaningful. Bored or angry with what they glimpsed, they started out to experiment on their own, in search of more satisfying values. In rapid succession, they tried and discarded Zen Buddhism and existentialism, occult and bizarre concepts in literature and the movies, "exploration of inner space" and the avant-garde in music (one example of which consisted of two minutes of silence, with the pianist sitting by the open grand piano), paintings of empty space "White on White" and the "Theater of the Absurd."

The indignities of making a living, long rejected by Dada, were fused with mystical psychologies and drugs; alcohol, marihuana, and LSD were all proclaimed as artificial paradises. Since rationality offered no challenge, the cult of nonsense was promulgated and copied; horror and violence were embraced as way-out status symbols. And all the time prosperity continued, with business taking full advantage of fourteen billion dollars a year "teen-age earnings and income."

*Look* magazine recently pointed out[9] that teen-agers have "arrived" as an economic force. The young people, a market of twenty-two million, are wooed and catered to by manufacturers and advertisers. The "Fastback," for example, was not so named by the auto manufacturers to please Grandfather; nor was one car named, ironically, "Rebel" for the older set.

Being an economic force is the one area in our affluent society where the young people could arrive—as consumers—but this technocratic egalitarianism has not provided any answer for their needed search for meaning. As some of them meet in their new roles—and this will be the last of the role playing, as we pointed out in the previous chapter—many feel that as young adults they are but ciphers on an IBM tape. Floating without a compass, faced with the colossus of the "multiversity," imprisoned in the knowledge of factories, some of them have banded together and cried out: "Do not fold, spindle or mutilate—us!"

They are orderly and less promiscuous than their older siblings were one generation ago. They are ready to fight for civil rights (following up in vigorous action the historic Supreme Court decision of 1954). They are skeptical about their elders' exported wars in various spots of the globe, explained with the slogan, "danger of communism." They are young, but they are adults, and they have not forgotten McCarthy and his excuse for the rise to tyranny; their parents have fought in a war against fascism and, unlike some of us who close our eyes, many of them are realistic enough to recognize that one third of their world has become a socialist world, quite different from theirs, and that the difference between the two worlds cannot be settled by wars or hydrogen bombs any longer.

Those of us who want to understand these young adults are faced with a considerable difficulty: the necessity to listen to a language we have never learned. Most of us have lived with the certainty of our values, and will not find it easy to understand a generation that is skeptical toward any of the possible solutions that our world has had to offer up to now. Young adults are skeptical toward free enterprise as well as socialism, toward passive resistance and toward violent revolution. They are skeptical and cautious because they are well aware that a few false decisions in some headquarters can mean the end of the human race. They sense that mankind may have come to the end of the road and that they may be the last generation. Theirs is the most awesome responsibility of all.

Not every young adult is fully aware of his historic role, but some are very conscious of it. Those who are most concerned both about their identity and their self-image, on the one hand, and about the world in which they hope to go on living, on the other, speak up, stage protest marches and sit-ins. If one wants to help, he will have to learn to listen to them, the way they themselves see their behavior and the society. One graduate student who had participated in one of the sit-ins at one of our large universities had this to say:

For all our lives we have been trained to believe in certain things. The training is largely nominal, but sometimes it penetrates. The sit-in was an ultimate petition . . . after all the formal avenues of redress had been tried: consulted, petitioned, sent letters, picketed, editorialized, waited, negotiated. For the past five years my political activity had been limited to occasional participation in Civil Rights pickets . . . I have chosen for five years simply not to be particularly involved, most of my friends share this pattern of casual and occasional involvement. My interest in the student Civil Rights movement has come . . . from its connection with and effect upon other aspects of our lives: in particular, our education and sense of community. I had been teaching assistant in Statistics and teaching Community Development for the Peace Corps and had neither the time nor the inclination to become involved . . . I am left personally with a renewed or perhaps new sense of belief in certain abstractions: freedom of political and other expressions, academic freedom, the idea of an intellectual community involved in a broad and common endeavor. And with a belief in the goodness of people that I did not, I think, have before, for I had never seen it demonstrated as I think it was among us . . . 15,000 students who comported themselves with dignity and grace, and with good hearts and trust and kindness for each other . . .

How do adults react to these words? With enthusiasm or indignation, admiration or pity? Is the writer of the statement right? Is he distorting the situation? Does he, indeed, represent the troubled young adult, or is he helping himself and discovering the "goodness in people"?

We do not know in each case whether participation in social action represents an inner disturbance or a healthy reaction to a disturbed society. For Tom Tibbett the work with the civil rights group on his campus was constructive social action, while his own identity dilemma continued to trouble him. The two pieces of behavior were not directly related, just as there is no simple, direct relationship between the troubled environment and the troubled individual. Some young adults protect themselves from the environmental disturbances by avoiding all contact with social conflicts. Other young people find solutions for themselves through involvements in groups.

There is a large body of opinion in the area of solutions, which deals with social organizations of young people, the modification of stress, and the changing of social power relationships in a given community. The field of sociology, in particular the growing body of research in group dynamics, as well as social group work and community organization, are pointing to new solutions for young people.

This body of knowledge falls outside the focus of this book, which is limited to solutions through individual help. In this sense we are talking only about "some" solutions in the following section, in which we attempt to clarify further some aspects of the helping process.

### In Brief:

The young adults of this generation have been drafted as pioneers in a Space Age during a crucial decade of our history, in which basic values have undergone radical changes. While the young adults lived through the period of the Cold War, they were not fully aware of the new historic roles in which society had cast them. As they enter young adulthood, they find the horizon overcast in an affluent society, leaving them to search for a more meaningful world of their own.

# PART III

# Some Solutions

# 10

# The Three R's of Helping

Before the helping process can begin, the young adult in trouble will have to recognize that he has a problem, be ready to do something about it, and be able to form a relationship with the helping adult. *Recognition, Readiness,* and *Relationship* are as much three fundamentals in the individual helping situation, as readin', ritin', and 'rithmetic are in education.

Our awareness of somebody else's difficulties, our skill and training, or our compassion do not substitute for these three basic conditions. It is perhaps one of the most frustrating experiences for a parent or a professional to visualize clearly a path of destruction for a young person in front of him, and to know that there is truly nothing one can do—unless these three conditions are met—not one, nor two, but all three.

And it does not matter whether we are a parent or a minister, a teacher or a psychiatrist, a social worker or a counselor; nobody can truly help another person before that person can face at least one aspect of his problem, no matter how minute. He has to be ready to do something about it, perhaps no more than make a

113

phone call, and face the difficulty of forming a special relationship, set up for the functioning of the helping process.

If these three basic conditions are met, we do not necessarily succeed with our help, but we have an even chance to work together.

### Recognition

Recognition requires some degree of self-awareness, enough of the ego structure to distinguish clearly between self and others, and between the early childhood aspect and the grown-up parts of one's self. Clearly, the infant can not have much self-awareness because the concept of his own self, as distinguished from others, is not yet well developed. He can feel pain and pleasure, but he does not know what caused the pain. The infant assigns the cause of pain to the outside world, which comes out in the phrase, "It's all your fault," a few years later, if the ego has not grown successfully.

If the ego fails to develop—although the body and parts of the intellect may—the grown person cannot have any recognition. He has remained emotionally on the level of the very young child, unable to see where he is causing himself pain, unable to separate inside and outside, completely self-involved, treating the outside world as a mirror in which he sees himself reflected, and believing still—as he did in infancy—that others exist only for one purpose: to meet his needs.

When he is uncomfortable, when he cannot do his work, cannot form relationships, cannot love, he will—as the small child—look, not to his own self for the causes, but to people, things, and events outside himself. He has no in-sight, he can only look out. He has no recognition, and cannot face any problems in himself. He expects somebody to take away the pain or the problem—as parents had done to some extent in early childhood—and will get very angry if his expectations are not met.

In other people, the disappointment in the outside world will not lead to anger, but to withdrawal. They will say that nobody cares about them, which is perfectly true, since they can not care for anybody else. But this reason is not recognized. Nothing is recognized objectively. The self-pitying individual feels like the neglected child, and often has been a neglected child. In a way, he is still waiting for the care and comfort he never had.

Fortunately, most people in their late teens and young adulthood, have a glimpse of self-awareness, some recognition that there may be something wrong in the way they are acting, in the way they are relating—that the trouble is not entirely in the outside world.

Take Mark Metcalf, for example. Supported by his father in his fantasy-belief that there was nothing wrong with him, Mark could not consider his inner self as a factor in his actions, but usually blamed others for whatever trouble he got into—girls or teachers or "bad luck" or his mother. Like the small child who assigns the bad things, the painful experiences, to parents or the "bad chair" he bumped into, Mark did not see what he was doing when a girl got pregnant. He saw only his success in school and in the store, and warded off, with a psychological blind spot, what he could not admit or face. The word "could" is emphasized here, to underline the fact that he was not able to recognize his own behavior. It is helpful to remain aware of the fact that it takes a certain amount of strength, some intact parts of the ego, to face the weaknesses.

Where the ego is very weak, any recognition is warded off or put off as long as possible, but even Mark eventually showed enough resilience to consider his own behavior as the possible cause of trouble, after he got caught in camp and was confronted by the camp director. It was as though he had bumped into that "bad chair" time and time again, and one day reconsidered and said to himself: "Maybe it is not the chair that causes the hurt on my leg, but the way I walk or fail to look." In other words, he began to internalize the problem, instead of continuing to externalize it and make believe that it was all coming from the bad environment.

In terms of the helping process, one may say that the camp director's confrontation of his behavior "helped" Mark to recognize the fact that he had some problems. But how much help had this confrontation really been? Would it not be more realistic to say that this had been a first step, which, by itself, could not lead to real help and change, unless a young man like Mark could also meet the other conditions: readiness to do something about the recognized problem, and the ability to form some relationship with the helper.

If you had talked to Susan Spencer, and asked whether she thought that smoking marihuana was good for her, she would most likely have smiled in her charming way and told you that she "knew" that turning on was "an escape and all that." Should one call this kind of "knowing" a real recognition of one's problems? Is this perhaps just another way of avoiding facing anything, through a kind of pseudo-recognition, which looks and sounds like understanding? Particularly in adolescence, but also in young adulthood, this kind of intellectual "knowing" is frequently used to ward off further any kind of recognition. By announcing that "I know" or "I know all about it," one blocks any further discussion or exploration, almost as if to announce: "There is nothing further to be said about it. Let's change the topic."

This is more or less abstract knowledge, detached from feelings and deeper meaning. We may call it cognition, without discernment by the emotions, as contrasted to recognition.

We should then think of degrees of recognition, of awareness, of insight, even in the initial stages of the helping process. Of course, as in other mental processes, the test of the depth of recognition will be in the action taken. We are familiar with surface expression, as distinguished from the ones that have genuine feelings attached to it. Certain people will, when we run across them, assure us that they have thought about calling us a dozen times in the past year. This is like Susan's "I know I have problems." If the acquaintance had meant it, why hasn't he called? If Susan had really known that drugs are dangerous, why hadn't she talked to somebody about the problem?

In other words, true recognition is usually proven by the next condition: the readiness to do something about it. There often is a time lag between these two steps which is difficult to evaluate. There may be moments of recognition, flashes of insight which are not yet strong enough to lead to a readiness for action, and often there is a vacillation between the desire to do something about a problem, and the wish to "forget about it"—which is how the problem started in the first place—by forgetting.

## Readiness

Mark Metcalf did make an appointment with a therapist, went a few times, and quit. He is a good example of young people who are not ready for help. Most family agencies have substantial files of cases known as "Brief Service" or "Diagnostic Service Only," as the child guidance clinics used to label them. Counseling agencies have rooms full of files of applicants who did not return. Clergymen have a substantial share of missed or cancelled appointments.

Not one of these thousands of cases is like any other of course, but most have one factor in common: in one way or another, they were not *ready* for working on their problems for more than a few hours. Did they waste their time, the worker's time, the agency's time? Not at all. The brief consultation was most important to them at the time and represented one step in the direction of facing their problems. Many people begin with a brief exploration. Some of them have come back five, or even ten years later, and have referred to the one visit which had been meaningful to them.

Since the concept of "readiness" is crucial to the understanding of the helping process, we might consider the term briefly for a fuller comprehension of the dynamics. As the popular use indicates, in *"getting* ready," we are dealing actually with a process, and not with a static fact.

Getting ready for an appointment will only be a problem if one has mixed feelings about it. If he has changed his mind, after he had agreed to be ready at eight o'clock for a meeting, he will be in conflict and possibly not be ready in time.

In other words, the motivation is related to the readiness. This is particularly crucial when it comes to the wish to be helped. Most people have mixed emotions about getting help and experience an initial difficulty in getting ready to make contact with a therapist or counselor.

After he has recognized that he has problems, he may hesitate before he is ready to do something about it. He may feel, "I should call the doctor or the minister or the family agency," but he does not necessarily act. He is not quite ready.

In other words: he is involved in an inner conflict about seeking help. One part of himself knows that he does have problems for

which professional help is needed; another part pulls in the opposite direction: doubt, rationalization, postponement, various excuses. He knows he should make that appointment, but doesn't feel
like it. We may put it in other words: one part pulls forward
toward working out the problems, toward reality, toward growth;
the other part pulls back, toward fantasy, toward earlier satisfac-
tions of the moment, toward more childlike gratifications.

These two parts of the psyche exist in all of us. Most of the time
they are in balance, but when it comes to an experience which is
new or frightening or difficult, such as seeking help, many people
experience an acute conflict. They are considering getting ready to
do something about their problems. The crucial test is whether one
actually picks up the phone and makes that call, or instead keeps
postponing it from month to month.

Just before a person picks up the phone, he experiences a great
many complex emotions and bewildering thoughts. The conflict has
been heightened, reached an inner climax, and nears resolution.
Once he has made the call, he feels somewhat relieved for the moment and, although he sometimes plays with the idea of changing
his mind and canceling, he will keep the date, like most people who
voluntarily call for an appointment.

If these conflicts are true for most of us, it is easy to understand
how much more difficult it is for those young adults who procrasti-
nate and postpone habitually, and still have to wrestle internally
with the many factors characteristic of this phase of growth, as
detailed in an earlier chapter.

Parents and friends of the post-adolescent have often asked
whether or not they could help him to get ready to make that appointment, or have offered to make it for him. What can any one
do who sees a young man or woman in trouble, who has begun to
recognize some of his problems, but is not really getting ready to
do anything about it? For one thing, we can agree with him that he
has problems and assure him that he can solve them. We can also
tell him about the available resources: the phone number of the
family agency, the private therapist, the counselor, or the minister.
We may do this once or twice, but it will not help to go on repeating it every few weeks. Having said it once, clearly and simply, we

can be assured that the young person knows about it and can use it if he is ready. Pushing will only make him angry and more resistant.

We can do more. We can help him to get ready by channeling all his requests for help to that source suggested once before: If we don't pinch-hit as a helper, the young person will experience more acutely the necessity of calling the professional source.

This will require restraint and discipline on our part, because it may seem to us as though we are being cold and unfriendly. In reality, we are more helpful if we let his tension build up, so that he feels more of a necessity of seeing the professional worker. Of course, this applies only to those young people who have already recognized the problem (condition one) and who have considered getting ready to do something about it, with a clear knowledge of the source of help—at least a phone number, and possibly the name of the worker or the agency.

Until the young person who is getting ready to act, feels the necessity for it, he will not move, but remain in that vague state of abstract recognition. Necessity means that there is just a little more discomfort than gratification in the infantile pleasures. As long as the alcoholic gets more satisfaction than discomfort—on balance —from drinking, he will not act to get himself straightened out. Readiness to do something about problems means the pain-pleasure balance must have tipped, with the pain or the discomfort being stronger than the infantile pleasures.

That he has recognized the problem means he has begun to tip the balance somewhat. If, in the internal struggle, the healthy forces grow from this awareness, he will get ready to act, and at least make a phone call to a helping source.

## Relationship

The third condition for the helping process is the most difficult one to meet, because it involves a relationship with another person, while until now (in recognition and readiness) he struggled with himself. Now he goes to the counselor, the caseworker at the family agency, the clergyman. He has some definite feelings and ideas about this person, even before he has met him, and the closer he gets to the office door, the more he regrets ever having gotten started on this course.

Some people believe that it is easier to talk about one's problems to somebody one knows well—an old acquaintance of the family, or a teacher. Actually, this is not realistic. With this old friend, one has built up a definite relationship in which one has been rather friendly, intelligent, and cooperative. These nice aspects of the friendly relationship may turn out to be handicaps when it comes to airing recently recognized problems, infantile gratifications, less rational feelings, and many fantasies.

The better the individual knows the helper before the helping relationship is started, the more difficult it is to talk freely, to expose weaknesses, to show the sides of the personality which one had been hiding from oneself before the recent recognition. It is less embarrassing to undress—mentally or physically—in front of a strange doctor than a father or an uncle who is a doctor. With a stranger, the atmosphere is neutral, friendly, and professional, and one has no disturbing memories of good times together at very different occasions. It is the same with baring one's emotional or mental troubles.

But let us assume that a young woman does not mind talking very freely to somebody she has known well, that she does not get embarrassed very easily, that she feels comfortable talking to somebody she trusts from past contacts. Even in this case, the past contacts will act as interferences. She will, without meaning to or even being fully aware, tailor-make her remarks to fit the image of the man to whom she is talking, because she knows his reactions, his likes and dislikes, and everybody wants to be liked, particularly when one talks about one's own problems.

If the man is a friend of her parents, and particularly likes her father, the young woman will not be as frank and acid in her expression of hostile feelings as she would be with somebody who has never met her family. As she is talking about her resentment against her father, she cannot help knowing that the counselor is a friend of his. She will soften what she feels and be less than direct and straightforward.

If she knows that the counselor is against premarital intercourse, she will not find it easy to tell him about her anxiety over pregnancy or the family's finding out.

The more one knows about the counselor, the more one will censor, knowingly or unknowingly. This is only natural, and should be expected.

There is also the unexpressed, but annoying suspicion that some of what she says may get back to the family, directly or inadvertently. The counselor or therapist may assure her that what she talks about is strictly confidential, but since he is a friend of the family, her parents may want to ask him, and what will he say?

While the initial part of a professional discussion with a familiar counselor is more pleasant than that with a total stranger, on balance this first agreeable feeling is not worth the price one pays in terms of involuntary censorship and unrecognized doubts about the confidentiality of the relationship.

The good, trusted family friend may be an excellent person to build the bridge to a professional stranger, provided this trusted friend sees the person in trouble once or twice, to ease him into a treatment or counseling relationship, but if it becomes more than that, young people, in particular, will refuse to move on and will insist that they continue to talk to "Bill," whom they say they trust.

If "Bill's" vanity is aroused and he feels that he is irreplaceable, the only one who can help this young person, the chances for a sound professional relationship are pretty well lost.

What about this crucial issue of trust, which will be on top of the list of difficulties in meeting the third condition of the helping process, the establishing of a relationship with the professional?

Let us acknowledge that it is unrealistic to expect a person in trouble—particularly a young person—to walk into an office he has never seen, sit down in front of a man or woman he has never met in his life, and be able to trust this stranger. Trusting, like any other feeling, involves a great many conscious and, particularly, unconscious emotions, only some of which are accessible to awareness, by definition.

The individual will have a reaction to the counselor, based on his personality, and based on his own needs and wishes. What the counselor looks like, how he sounds, how he speaks, the language he uses, his voice, the way he is dressed, the looks of his office, his manner as he answers a telephone call—these and many other visible aspects will play a part in determining the troubled young person's feelings. Then, there are less obvious aspects—the kind of questions he asks or doesn't ask, his reactions to what the young person says, his explanations or hunches—these are more factors that determine trust, or lack of it.

But perhaps the most significant reactions are not the conscious ones, but those which the young person may not perceive in the beginning, but which may dawn on him much later. Long before one sees the counselor or therapist, one has an idea of what this person will be like: he will be a benign or a critical figure, an all-understanding or wise man, a know-it-all, or a seductive charmer, somebody one can fool, or somebody who sees straight through you.

Depending on the guilt, the particular personality, and the background of the person who goes for help, the image of the counselor or caseworker will change. If the young person feels guilty about many of his problems and the therapist asks, "Why?" he will take this, not as an inquiry, but as a criticism. Instead of reacting to a question, he will react as if he had been told, "You shouldn't have done that." In other words, he will give the professional certain qualities that other counseling figures have had in his life—pre-eminently parents, who were the first counselors and teachers.

He will do this without conscious awareness, but by virtue of the fact that he is repeating a very familiar situation from early childhood, where he was in need of help and went to powerful-seeming parents who were there to help him. He may be older than the counselor, the counselor may be a man—he may still unconsciously react as if he were reacting to his mother, the way he did when he was small.

This has more to do with trust than with the conscious and surface observations, what one may have heard about the therapist, or the degrees on his wall.

Of course, it helps if one can feel comfortable with a stranger; this ability, or lack of it, is often also a guide for the choice of the therapist or counselor. This will be a factor if one chooses a private, rather than a public helping source, such as a clinic or a social agency, which is often privately supported, but cannot give its clients the choice of the worker. People who are looking for a private therapist, cannot always know how to make such a choice, and will do better asking their doctor or minister, the family caseworker or guidance counselor, for advice.

Some young people may have to see several therapists or counselors before they find the one who is right for them, but if nobody is right, the problem has most likely to do with condition three, the ability to form a professional relationship. It would be another way of expressing the hesitation of translating both recognition and readiness into concrete action.

Susan Spencer is a case in point. We recall how she reacted to her guidance counselor's suggestion that she get some help. At first, she made fun of it to her friends, later, she did consider the idea when her mother had several talks with her, and eventually, she saw a very good caseworker in a family agency for a few sessions. Susie was pleasant and cooperative on the surface, seemed not to mind talking about herself, the school troubles, the smoking of marihuana, the sexual promiscuities. In fact, she admitted later that she got a "kick" out of "shocking" the "lady-doctor," as she named the caseworker.

Susie took pride in her behavior and seemed to agree that this is not very desirable behavior for most people, except that it was all right for her. She never made contact with the professional worker, but "sounded off," as she would with a group of friends, or as she once had on a television program where she was a discussant of "teen-age problems." While the caseworker was trying to understand Susie, the young woman did all she could to hide, both from herself and from the worker, her feelings of emptiness, desperation, and depression. She made it her business to sound "cool," detached, and very critical about "the establishment."

While everybody will instinctively avoid bringing up difficult material, there is a world of difference between a young woman who has difficulties remembering very much or talking altogether, and a Susan Spencer, who has not really experienced much internal conflict, who has almost a satisfactory adjustment to her illness and gets more gratification from being "crazy" or "sick" than from functioning at her best.

It may take even the most skilled professional several intensive sessions with a young man before he can know with any degree of certainty to what extent this patient can indeed enter into a therapeutic or helping relationship. This explains the many brief service cases, or the "consultation only" cases referred to before. But we should also realize that the majority of people who have a recognized problem, and are ready to do something about it, have the determination to form this new and often difficult relationship with a professional person.

The overcoming of hesitation to enter into this relationship is already part of the process of change, which is always necessary if one really wants to help himself.

### In Brief:

Regardless of our desire to help young people, and quite aside from our training, gift, and skill, we should recognize that the helping process hinges on three conditions which all have to exist for the young person if one hopes to effect some changes. They are:

*Recognition:* enough self-awareness to be able to consider the inner causes of one's problems, in contrast to the earlier tendency to blame them on parents or somebody in the world outside.

*Readiness:* the ability to translate recognition into some concrete action, aimed at "doing something" about the problems.

*Relationship:* enough readiness to overcome the natural hesitation to share with a professional person those aspects of one's personality that one had hidden from oneself, until the recent recognition.

# 11

# Parents of Troubled Youth

Unless they are too frightened to face their own problems, many parents of young people in trouble look for clarification or guidance for themselves. Some talk to their family physician, who may suggest a psychotherapist, while others seek counsel from their clergyman or a family agency. Frequently parents meet in groups to discuss their youngsters and their own roles. They may get together in a church, a family agency, an adult education center, a clinic. Often they have the guidance of a professional worker, trained in helping people through the medium of the group.

After the natural hesitation to share their troubles with others, parents experience relief and comfort from recognizing that other people have trouble too. "I am not the only one" is a common feeling for all of us which often makes it possible to face difficulties with less guilt and anxiety.

What is such an experience like? Does it help parents to help their young people? Can we learn from them by looking in on such a group?

Take the parents of the six young people whom we met earlier, and imagine them in a group session at a moment of crisis, when their children's troubles are alarming.

There would be *Mr. and Mrs. Tibbett,* while Tom is in jail, following his sit-in demonstration near college.

Sitting next to them could be *Mrs. Lewis,* terribly concerned about Linda, her beautiful daughter, now living with another girl in a lesbian relationship.

*Mr. and Mrs. White* might have taken time out from the store, very troubled about their only boy Walt, who is home, sitting in the back room drawing and reading by the hour and talking to nobody.

125

*Mr. and Mrs. Grant* would have driven in from their farm, very angry and upset about Gwen, who not only is downhearted all the time, but now has screamed at the teacher, after having stopped in the middle of her final examination.

The reluctant husband and the interested wife are *Mr. and Mrs. Metcalf,* who have come after Mark has finally been expelled from the camp where he was a swimming counselor, following his indiscretion with one of the campers.

Sitting by herself, probably, is *Mrs. Spencer,* completely at a loss as to what to do with Susie, who not only smokes pot, stays out all night, and does no work in school, but also seems not to be the least bit concerned about anything she does.

This could well be a group of troubled parents of youth in trouble—the Tibbetts, Mrs. Lewis, and the Whites on one side of the table, and opposite, the Grants, the Metcalfs, and Mrs. Spencer.

The group leader at the head of the table—let's call him Mr. Turner—has identified himself, introduced the parents to each other, and put them all at ease. He has presented the topic for discussion: clarification of the troubles of their children and ways to understand and help them.

## A Group Session

Mrs. Spencer, who arrived last, is the first to speak, after Mr. Turner asks for participation. She shocks some of the parents as she describes Susie's experiences with marihuana.

"You mean to sit there and tell us that this kind of thing goes on in your own house?" Mr. Tibbett asks with indignation.

Mrs. Spencer shakes her head. It does not happen at home, but she has seen Susie come home "high," frightfully elated, "like a rubber doll," and inaccessible to reason. "I have found some of this stuff in her night-table drawers," she goes on. "I threw it in the toilet, but a week later there was some more!"

"Where is she getting it?" Mrs. Metcalf wants to know. "This sort of thing costs money!"

Mr. Grant, as indignant as Mr. Tibbett, declares that this is a matter for the police. "It's against the law," he says factually, fold-ing his gnarled hands and sitting back, having said all there is to say.

Several of the parents nod assent, except Mrs. White, who shakes her head vehemently. "Putting 'em in jail won't help," she declares firmly. "They'll come out confirmed criminals."

Mrs. Lewis, thinking of Linda and laws against homosexuality, agrees timidly. "I wouldn't want it on my conscience," she says, "to have my daughter accuse me of having put her in prison."

Mr. White, wondering how widespread the habit is, wants to know whether Mrs. Lewis' daughter is taking drugs also.

"No," Mrs. Lewis replies, "Linda has other problems."

Now Mr. Turner, the leader, intervenes, both to save Mrs. Lewis embarrassment and to bring the group back to the topic. "Young people sometimes get in trouble with the law for many different reasons," he says, "while they are experimenting and trying things out for size."

Mr. Tibbett raises his hand. "It's the parents' job to stop them," he declares, "no matter how! Laws must be respected!"

"It depends," a timid voice comes in, and to everybody's surprise, it turns out to belong to the wife of the man who has just spoken. "Sometimes laws are wrong," Mrs. Tibbett insists. "My son is in jail right now for a sit-in demonstration, and I must say I'm proud of him!"

There is a moment of significant silence, as the parents think this over. They also cannot help noticing the open split between the parents of the boy who is in jail.

"There is a difference between taking dope and protesting an injustice," Mr. White says calmly. "I think it isn't fair to put them all together."

The leader, wanting as much participation as possible now, turns to Mr. Metcalf and Mrs. Grant, both of whom have not said a word. What do they think of this issue?

Mr. Metcalf smiles a little, embarrassed because he would have preferred to say nothing, but he agrees that there are two sides to every question. "Besides," he continues, "we have a very different problem with our boy. Girl-crazy, you know."

His wife interrupts, with some defiance and anger. " 'Girl-crazy' isn't the word," she says. "Mark got two girls pregnant and has taken no responsibility for it. His latest is being kicked out of camp for sleeping with one of the campers. He was a counselor. I wouldn't call this just 'girl-crazy.' "

Mrs. Grant folds her arms across her chest and lets out a long sigh. "I think kids don't have enough discipline these days. They all think the world owes them a living. If you ask me, they should all have been spanked when they were little. No discipline. That's all."

The leader notices some parents smiling at the last remark and suggests that perhaps many things should have been handled differently when these young adults were small, but now they are big, eighteen and older, and what can the group do to help them?

There is a long silence, with every parent looking to the others for answers.

"To tell the truth," Mrs. White finally says, "there isn't too much you can do when they get that big. They're practically grown people . . ."

Mr. Tibbett clears his throat. "They still come to us for money," he announces. "That's one important hold we have on them. They'd like to act independent, but let's be realistic—who pays the bills?"

Mrs. Grant shakes her head decisively. "I'm paying no bills for a kid of mine," she says. "If Gwen can't finish school, she'll go to work, or I'll know the reason why! 'If you're old enough to scream at the teacher,' I told her, 'you're old enough to work at the mill.' "

The leader asks for a comment on this method.

"You don't give her a chance," Mrs. Spencer tells Mrs. Grant, "if you make her work full-time. Without an education, she can't get very far."

Mr. Grant is thinking this over and trying to back up his wife. "You've got to earn the right for an education," he says. "Nobody handed me anything. You work. In school or in a job. That's all there is to it."

"In a way I agree with the gentleman," Mr. Tibbett chimes in. "I told Tom either he cuts out the nonsense in that college of his or he comes home and goes to school where we live. Parents have some rights, as long as they pay the bills."

Mr. Turner looks at Mrs. Lewis for a comment, but instead of speaking, she begins to cry, softly and with shame. She apologizes and explains that she has been thinking about Linda and the "unbelievable thing" this beautiful girl has done to her, a devoted mother.

After some of the parents have soothed Mrs. Lewis, Mrs. Tibbett expresses a feeling that is common, judging by the silent approval, when she says: "Your daughter's problem seems the worst in the world, and to me, Tom's troubles are heartbreaking. I could understand your daughter if I knew her, and you could probably help my son better than I can right now."

All the parents feel reassured when the group leader tells them that very frequently young people find it easier to confide in adults other than those in their own family. "Still," he goes on, "you have come here to see how you can be of the most help to your own young people, and perhaps we could talk about one or two of them in more detail so that we can understand the problem and perhaps be of help to one another."

The first parent to speak up, after the hesitation, is Mark's mother, Mrs. Metcalf, who tells simply and directly about her son.

The group gets two sides of the story because Mark's mother emphasizes his sexual problems, the trouble he has gotten into at home and in camp, while his father tells of the young man's good reputation on the job, his fair marks in college, and his friendliness around the house.

"He is supposed to see a doctor," Mrs. Metcalf concludes, "and he *will* do it, but I don't think he will go more than once. He doesn't want to go, to tell the truth."

When the leader asks for comments, Mr. Tibbett raises his hand. "Frankly," he says, "after listening to the boy's father, I'm not surprised at anything!"

Replying to the startled inquiries from the other parents, Tom's father explains that he has gotten the idea that Mr. Metcalf seems to be almost proud of his boy's delinquencies, the way he is defending him, and doesn't seem to see anything wrong with his way of acting.

"That's ridiculous!" Mr. Metcalf booms, but there is not much anger in his voice.

Mr. Grant too thinks that this is something a boy gets from his father, "men's business," something that can't happen if a boy respects his father.

Both Whites disagree violently, siding with Mrs. Spencer, who wants to know why nobody is blaming the girls who have gotten involved with Mark.

"From what you have told us about your daughter," Mr. Metcalf says, "you don't seem to have had much influence on her either."

The group is agitated. Charges and countercharges are flying; instead of talking about ways to help their children, the parents are discussing their own problems quite openly.

Not until Mrs. Tibbett speaks does the tension subside. "The longer I listen to this discussion," she says in her timid voice, "the more I'm convinced that we're the last people on earth to offer any advice to our children. Our time is past, it seems to me. We had our chance and muffed it. All we can do now is hope and pray."

Although her husband disagrees vehemently, her words have influenced the group. There are many comments, elaborating on her point.

"My advice to you," Mrs. Tibbett says, "is to remain on good terms with your grown children. We have lost our son for good, just because we insisted that he do what we tell him. I'm sorry now, because nothing is worse than to talk to your own son and daughter-in-law as if you're talking to strangers. I can't explain it, but if you lose this something you have had with your children, you might as well move to Arizona and retire or fade out. It's the worst thing that can happen to a parent. Believe me."

Before the leader has a chance to summarize, Mrs. Metcalf speaks up, disagreeing heartily with Mrs. Tibbett.

"I think that's a lot of foolishness," she says. "My husband is on very good terms with Mark. A lot of good it did him! I was the one who tried to teach him right and wrong, and me he hates!"

Mrs. Tibbett explains that she does not mean "peace at any price, but 'coexistence,' to use words from the family of nations."

The leader uses this last, conciliatory remark to pull together some of the things that have been discussed, and, expressing his hope that the parents would meet again to get into more details, ends their meeting.

## Some Lessons for Parents

What can we learn from listening to a meeting like this and similar attempts to arrive at some solutions? Parents the country over sit up many a long evening to try to figure out how they can be of more help to their children. There are thousands of adult education classes for parents, many meetings like this one, in very different settings. Some groups meet to arrive at practical solutions, others are set up for the purpose of helping parents solve some of their own problems: parents' counseling, group work with parents, group therapy for selected members of families—a great many, different attempts to find answers for troubled youth and troubled families.

From all this, a few lessons seem to emerge, even though they are necessarily general.

1. *The role of parents is sharply limited when their children are grown.*

Even when young people have no particularly complicated problems, the relationship to their parents is one of coexistence, as Mrs. Tibbett said in the meeting. Parents and young adults do not always have too much in common nowadays, and they often get along in a state of civilized detachment. While both generations try their best somehow to maintain the illusion of the original family, neither parents nor young people really believe that this is genuine any longer. The roles have gradually and subtly changed, barely noticed at first, grudgingly acknowledged later, and finally, reaching a point where little of the original relationship is left. Unless young people and their parents can rediscover each other, the way one discovers people one has barely known at a party, unless they can like each other as interesting people with common ideas and interests, unless both young people and parents can let go of the past and the age differences and become friends on the same equal basis on which one makes friends with anybody one likes very much, there can be no meaningful relationship between young people and their parents.

This rediscovery is difficult to achieve and requires constant work on the part of both parties. Often either parents or young people slip back into the old roles, reawakening old conflicts and positions, and with them, states of hostile dependency—"I don't like you because I need you"—states of open warfare or an uneasy peace, resembling a Cold War status.

In other words, both parents and young people have a difficult time trying to maintain contact. The reasons for this natural difficulty are well known and need only to be listed to be immediately recognized—ambivalence of love and hate; confusion of guilt and loyalties; unresolved incestuous conflicts, which are mostly unconscious and therefore not recognized; old aggressive or hostile remnants which can burst to the surface with seemingly no provocation; unresolved early competitive feelings between brothers and sisters on one side and mother or father on the other; unfulfilled dependency wishes emerging at sometimes the most inappropriate moment; repetition of behavior which is as irritating now as it was then—a host of accumulated emotions, thoughts, and habits, which may well interfere with a good, mature parent–young-adult relationship.

Where the ego of young people has been unable to mediate successfully between the myriad of early instinctual demands and the pressures of objective reality, where the young adult, as a result, has developed a host of substitute gratifications, known clinically as symptoms, or in plain language "trouble," the role of parents is much more limited. The deeper young people are in trouble, the more ineligible their parents are to take the role of helpers.

2. *The existence of an accepting family is vital for rehabilitation.*

Troubled young adults are often disturbed people who may require treatment, just as people with physical illness do. The treatment will be administered by professionals, but whether or not any patient will get well has a great deal to do with the home he can go back to. This is as true for psychosis as it is for pneumonia.

It is therefore vitally important that parents of troubled youth maintain good contact with their grown young people, a task that requires considerable self-restraint and patience on everybody's part. The solid contact must get priority over the concern about a shocking episode or act. Since young people may lose perspective in an emergent, desperate situation, it is that much more necessary for parents to keep a level head. Indeed, young people who have gone far away from their familes will return in moments of crisis if they can be sure that they will be welcomed, instead of criticized, berated, or ridiculed.

It is utterly useless to ask them, "Why did you do it?" because young people who have done great damage to themselves or others, will tell you, "I don't know." This is the very best answer they can give. It means, translated into behavorial language: "The motives for my action were not on the level of consciousness, even though I may seem to have known what I was doing." There are a great many levels of awareness and degrees of consciousness, and if young people tell us that they knew what they were doing, they are referring to intellectual knowledge. We can be quite sure that if they have done damage to themselves or others, their reality sense was not in full control, and some of the early instinctual demands have flooded the ego, leading to the acting-out which caused the trouble.

The interminable interrogations between parents and young people in trouble are of no help whatsoever. On the contrary, they damage the tenuous relationship further, sometimes to the point of no return, after which young people will be without any hope, and may become desperate and very dangerous.

Because youth in trouble reawaken the old, unresolved conflicts within the family—as we have noticed in the group session—it is important to guard against acting-out between the parents.

The sharp difference in attitudes toward the bringing up or the educating of children that was evident in the group session is not unusual in families where young people get into trouble. By making it possible for children to avoid their requests—which are often based on objective reality needs, not on arbitrary wishes, as children sometimes imagine—parents hamper their children from experiencing the boundaries of reality, of how far they can go in trying to get what they want at the moment. They get the impression in early childhood that with enough cunning, pleading, and crying, the parental requests can be avoided. The reality sense does not develop fully, and this is one of the factors that may get them into trouble later when they expect the same methods that have worked in the past at home to work again in school or the outside world.

When they are in trouble as young adults, it is only natural that they will try once more to get between the parents, and by playing one against the other, to get what they want at the moment, the same as long ago.

Of course, parents will have their own individual opinions and attitudes, but when it comes to making major decisions regarding their children, even in young adulthood, it helps if parents do not make their young people victims of powerful unresolved conflicts. Certainly, Mark Metcalf's resistance to therapy was encouraged by his father's attitude, and might have had less impact if both parents could have agreed that treatment was really necessary for a boy as disturbed as he.

If the Tibbets could have settled their differences before exposing them to Tom—who had his own conflicts—he would have been in a much better position to arrive at a mature decision regarding his personal and professional future. As it happened, his parents' sharply clashing viewpoints muddled his own confusion further, instead of clarifying it. This was the natural result of a family climate in which all basic conflicts were hushed up and covered with a cloak of refined, restrained liberalism, modulated voices, and avoidance of open differences at all costs. Because of this atmosphere, one could not expect Tom to be able to maintain any kind of meaningful relationship with his family, something that may well have made the difference between the road he felt he had to take and a happier life.

3. *In the strained parent–troubled-youth relationship, further tension can be prevented by:*

a. *Avoiding intellectual battles,* in which parents and young people often use each other as sparring partners. As has often been pointed out, these seemingly intelligent arguments generate much more heat than light, but if the combatants are parents and youth in trouble, the arguments do more than this. They become a disguise for exchanging hostile feelings under the cloak of intellectual differences. Both parties end up feeling more alienated than before the "discussion" started, a condition which is contrary to what young people need at a time of trouble. Whether the topic is politics, drama, sports, religion, economics, or music—if combustible, controversial issues can be avoided, both parents and troubled young people will benefit.

b. *Avoiding any provocation,* no matter in which form it is made. This is a time when troubled young people will—without meaning to—challenge their parents not only to intellectual duels, but to commitments, rejection, over-anxiety, unrealistic reactions. This will take the form, "You don't want me to become a street cleaner, do you?" to which the expected answer is, "Of course not," whereupon comes the clincher, "Then let me have the five hundred dollars to start my own business."

It may take other forms, "You promised that I could get my own apartment if I got a straight B average." The parent doesn't remember ever having made such a promise, but maybe he has. Perhaps a year ago, in a moment of weakness, he made such a commitment; perhaps he said only, "Maybe." Now that the young person is in trouble—and the adult is an understanding parent and thinks of trouble as illness—he feels he must not do anything to aggravate the problems further. He feels caught, troubled by a sense of guilt or anxiety, and he is most likely not able to be as realistic, as objective as he can be when he is at his best. He has been provoked, and may need time to reevaluate this request, perhaps to objectify it with a friend, perhaps with the young person's therapist or caseworker, if he or she is seeing somebody. If parents can take a reasonably firm stand at such moments and not allow themselves to be blackmailed, both the final decision and the relationship will be better.

c. *Avoiding moralizing where practical counsel is needed.* Let's take promiscuity as an example. When Mark Metcalf's mother first suspected he not only went out with two or three different girls, but also had intimate sexual relations with them, she sat him down for a long talk, the first of many. She told him the usual thing—that he was too young, not mature enough to have intimate relations, irresponsible, and not thinking of the girls—the Mother Lecture. Mark, as was his custom, listened and nodded politely and, as expected, went right on doing what he had done in the first place.

Susan's mother did not believe in Mother Lectures; she tried instead to limit Susie's going-out time, to check on where she went, and to make sure that she was at supervised parties—for a year or two. Although she had overheard Susie talk to girl friends on the phone, and had read that young girls, particularly insecure and anxious ones, try to feel more secure and grown-up by sleeping with boys or men, Mrs. Spencer chose not to know about it, for fear of finding out the truth. When Susie one day mentioned her sexual behavior in a casual, offhand manner, her mother was shocked, and forbade her to bring boys into the house, or to stay overnight at anybody's house. Susie, to provoke her mother, defied her to prove that she was wrong. Mrs. Spencer, cornered, said that there was nothing to talk about; it was altogether unspeakable.

When it looked several months later as though Susie were pregnant, Mrs. Spencer wished she had spoken about it—not by putting her foot down, which she knew by experience would not be any help at all, but by talking about protection against pregnancy!

This, at least, was what she felt would have been realistic after having seen a professional a few times, when she was so upset about Susie that she could not function either at home or on her job. This therapist suggested that she had better not try to deal with the causes of Susie's promiscuous behavior and her sexual acting-out, but should instead insist that the young woman see a gynecologist to have a diaphragm fitted or get birth-control pills. The time for moralizing was long past, he suggested, and what was needed now was both psychotherapy and realistic prevention of further damage.

Mrs. Spencer, like Mrs. Metcalf and many other parents, felt that this would be aiding behavior that they thoroughly disapproved of. This is a very understandable reaction on the part of parents, particularly at this time of history when so many basic values are confused, partially for cultural reasons.

This mode of thinking is like the one used in earlier childhood when parents avoid certain subjects, reasoning that talking about them "will put ideas into their heads." This is an overestimation of outside stimuli and a lack of respect for the individual's ability to cope with stimuli.

We do not put any ideas into anybody's head—whether he be a little child or a college student—by talking about something. For an idea to take root, there first has to be fertile soil; the individual has to be interested in our idea. If he is, talking about it can only clarify possible confusion. If he is not interested, he will do what we all do with things that do not interest us—screen it out. Perception is highly selective, and all we need to be concerned about is our sensitivity to the young person's response. If he is not interested, he will show it, and we don't go on and on with our favorite topic. If he is, we have a basis for a clarifying talk.

If Susie Spencer and Mark Metcalf are acting out their sexual confusion, we do not put ideas in their heads by talking about protection. Our indignation or disapproval will not protect them realistically. Nor will it help them with protection of the ego, the central inner coordinator. If they have not developed this protection of the ego by now, we cannot help them, but will need professionals to do the job.

"Avoiding moralizing where practical counsel is needed" applies, of course, to all areas of concern. We have used promiscuity as one example; it could have been confusion in direction of work or study, conflicts over relationship, or any other area. Nothing strains the parent–young-adult relationship further than the false kind of understanding which has become popular in the last ten years. A great many young people have expressed their rage about parents who continually "analyze everything I say," amateur psychologists who do not really try to listen and understand, but who get some gratification from having "the answer."

4. *If support—financial or moral—is to be effective, it has to be unconditional.*

The one hurdle which often proves to be the last, fatal one for parent-youth relationships is money. It is used either for emotional blackmail, a pet charity, or a handout, but only rarely as a realistic, objective means to help troubled young people. Both the giving and the withholding of money are fraught with a great number of emotions, past and present, of which guilt, hostility, and overindulgence are only a few visible signs. Money is used to manipulate, dominate, buy affection, induce guilt, control people's lives—often continuing beyond the parents' lifetime through the wording of the last will and testament.

Young people are often quite as unrealistic about money as parents, mainly because they have not been given the opportunity to grow naturally into experiencing the factual meaning of this form of exchange. Even in families where the parents earn enough money not to have to worry about it, young people frequently know much more about calculus than about mortgages, more about the autonomic nervous system than about hospitalization insurance, more about the cost of repairing the roof of their car than the roof of the house in which they have lived for the past twenty years. In brief, young people have frequently been kept economically ignorant, shielded from the realities of father's income and expenses (knowing at best one or the other, but seldom both), never been told about deductible items in a tax statement, the concept of a family budget, annuities, or savings.

When young people talk about their fathers, either in the present, or as they remember them from early childhood, they usually have not much more to say than the fact that "he worked." Where he went every day; what he actually did all day long; how much money he earned, by the hour, or by commission, or through a bonus; how he got his job; how he trained for his work; what it means—none of this is usually a realistic part of their thinking. Whatever the philosophy of these young people's parents, it is not helpful, because young people fail to experience gradual contact with the reality of the economy.

By the time they are young adults, they are quite suddenly expected by their parents to swim. Parents say, "Pay for this nonsense yourself," or, "How do you expect us to pay for this?" or, "You don't know the value of money." Quite suddenly, money—the last hold of the parents of troubled young people—is used to exert the last, desperate pressure, making it appear that money and work are quite similar to prison labor, and that working for a living is an altogether punitive exercise, to which youngsters usually react with the outcry, "Unfair!"

Gwen Grant, for example, was totally unprepared to make her own living, and would never have been thrust into this situation if she had not had difficulties in school. Tom Tibbett's life would never have taken the course it took if Mr. Tibbett had not used his ability to pay for college as a wedge to make Tom do what Father wanted. In the end, both of them lost. Tom got into permanent trouble, and Father lost his son. Mrs. Metcalf refused to pay for

Mark's motorcycle, as if money were the issue, thus confusing it completely in Mark's mind, for the boy got the idea that the motorcycle would be acceptable to his parents if he paid for it himself. We see how Mrs. Spencer was the one who was concerned with the expense of marihuana when she talked about it, again being preoccupied with money, while the real issue was Susie's depression, which she tried to avoid with drugs.

While young people are often encouraged to take part-time or even full-time jobs, on which they earn at times considerable amounts, the concept of "my own money" is not realistic while young people live and eat at home. With the basic expenses met by the family, their earnings are still a variation of the allowance. Walt White helped every day in his parents' store, waiting on customers and taking in change, without making any contact with reality—no more than small children who play store with toy money. When Linda Lewis worked in the acting studio—she was going on nineteen years then—she thought that two thousand dollars a year was a great deal of money, a fortune that she could never hope to amass or earn. When she heard what some accomplished colleagues earned and needed for a comfortable living, her reaction was, "That's for grown-ups." Just as she had not developed a realistic image of herself as a young adult, so she had no realistic concept of what it took to live by herself. This diffusion existed in Linda as well as in the five other young people, in spite of and independent of the fact that they were all very bright and scored above average in intelligence tests.

In the lives of all the young people, financial or moral support had not been effective and realistic because it had been given conditionally instead of factually. Mrs. Metcalf would have been more effective if she had taken a clear stand against motorcycles—quite aside from the question of who pays for it. If she believed that this was a wrong thing to buy, it remained wrong, whether she or Mark paid for it. When Mr. Tibbett declared that he would pay for college "only if" Tom stopped his community activities, he took the stance of a holdup man who enforces his will with a gun, and may be effective, but will be hated for his act. Gwen's mother was equally ineffective by giving Gwen the alternative—school or job— because the real problem was Gwen's long-standing sense of hopelessness, not an unwillingness to work. Like Mrs. Grant, many parents have the illusion that the way out of learning troubles is "to get a job."

Getting a job is difficult for many people, even when they have a definite skill, trade, or profession. The fear of being rejected, the uncertainty of meeting unknown people, the anxiety about one's ability to perform adequately—these are all factors that operate in many of us when we consider applying for a position.

The same problems exist in a much more serious way when the applicant has no skill or trade, when he has failed in his education or previous work attempts. If it is difficult to apply for a job as a salesman or a teacher, it is almost impossibly difficult to consider "a" job, any job, an unspecified, undefined, nameless spot somewhere in the world. If the young man felt downcast before, when he failed in school, he is bound to feel hopeless about the prospect of getting "a" job.

That some young people manage to overcome this dreary and impersonal situation is a victory for their endurance. It is usually a short-lived victory, because the same problems that stopped them from working with concentration in school, frequently will stop them also from performing on a job.

*In Brief:*

Parents of troubled youth often work on their own problems, in individual or group relationships. One parent-guidance session was illustrated from which a few lessons have been extracted. They are:

1. The role of parents is sharply limited when their children are grown.
2. The existence of an accepting family is vital for rehabilitation.
3. In the strained parent–troubled-youth relationship, further tension can be prevented by:
   a. Avoiding intellectual battles.
   b. Avoiding any provocation.
   c. Avoiding moralizing where practical counsel is needed.
4. If support—financial or moral—is to be effective, it has to be unconditional.

# 12

# Working With Troubled Youth

Before we consider some characteristics of those groups of people who have made working with troubled youth their profession, we should remember that the majority of young adults, with their own special problems, will not have any contact with professional workers. Most troubled young people will be left to their own resources, many will struggle to find their own solutions and in the process will get help for a time from many different people. Not only will they turn to the family physician and the clergyman, the law-enforcement officer and the intelligent neighbor, but many young people will get help from specialists in other fields.

There are many specialists in all the areas of sports, and there are the workers in the arts—painters and sculptors, musicians and dancers, writers and theater experts.

And, finally, there is the army of "just people," men and women in all trades and professions—businessmen and lawyers, farmers and craftsmen—a large, anonymous contingent of people who care for and are not afraid of troubled youth.

This, after all, is perhaps the primary requisite for people who want to work with troubled youth, in whatever capacity. The fear of troubled young people exists in many adults. We find such fear among psychiatric residents and psychological interns, among psychiatric social workers and nurses, group workers in settlement houses and camps, baseball coaches and high school teachers—in brief, the fear of adolescents or young adults exists in any profession or group of people.

These fears are not always recognized or acknowledged by adults, but are often denied and discharged in many forms of compensation: false chumminess, rigidity, overindulgence, frozen states of friendliness, search for the right distance—many expressions of uneasiness, which often contain fear or deeply hidden hostility. This may differ with feelings about young men or women, alone or in groups, but such feelings exist frequently and explain in part why even among the small number of professional people, there is an even greater dearth of specialists, ready and able to work with young people.

But professional or not, where the feelings of hostility exist, they will interfere in the teamwork between adults and youth. People are challenged or provoked by youth, intimidated or insulted; they say a group of eighteen-year-olds makes them feel like running away or brings out the drill sergeant in them—all kinds of strange reactions that these same people may not have with either small children or contemporaries.

Articulating reasons, even if we understood them, would not help, since no intellectual explanation of unconscious, or partially conscious feelings can change attitudes. We can say that youth often trigger in adults unexplained emotions from their own past, emotions that interfere, to some degree, with the adults' ability to work with any young person. Such emotions make it next to impossible for them to help troubled youth, young men and women who are particularly sensitive to hidden fears and hostilities in the adults in their lives.

## Who Can Work With Troubled Youth?

Since the transmission belt between adults and youth is *relationship,* not the activity they engage in together, it may be helpful to draw a theoretical profile of an adult who has the "ideal" personality for helping youth—quite apart from his intellectual or artistic training, his theoretical knowledge, or his acumen in the field of behavior.

We can attempt to develop this profile by first stating insignificant or negative factors that have no bearing.

## The Sex of the Adult Is Not Significant

For years, the idea that men should work with boys or young men, and women with girls or young women, dominated the thinking of the supervisors who assign cases in mental hygiene clinics, casework agencies, and camps. This thinking was based on a confused concept of "identification." It was also based on a naïve concept of substitution of missing figures in the family.

We have since learned from psychoanalysis that in the formative years when identification is the primary mode of relating, the individual sees the primary figures, not necessarily as they are, but as he needs to see them. Concepts, such as masculine and feminine, are not so much determined by biological characteristics as by behavior.

Every therapist has had a patient who thought of his or her mother as the one "who wore the pants in the family," the one who rewarded and punished, who said what was right and wrong, who controlled the allowance, the food, the routine of the household—who ran the show. To such a patient, Mother was the aggressor, the more "masculine," dominant member of the family, while Father often was associated with softness, gentleness—"feminine" attitudes.

For these patients, the traditional concept of "the man in the family" meant nothing, except a word or a piece of fiction from a movie or a story. In their world, the man in the family was very different from what they were told was "masculine." The resulting confusion about their own sexual identification was one of their problems, but should we assign to them as a helper a "man-worker" or a "woman-worker," without knowing what these concepts mean? If we don't know enough about the individual, we might ask him whom he would prefer. This may not be best for him, but it would be more informed than our cliché thinking about men and women.

## The Age of the Adult Is Not Significant

This is another criterion that was once erroneously used for bringing adults and youth together. As with sexual characteristics, people have their own, very individual reactions to chronological age, depending on their particular life experiences. For some young people, anybody over thirty is "square" and beyond the pale of communication. For others, people begin to count only after they have white hair and glasses, for only then have they had enough "experience" to be respected. One of the most successful teachers of a large class of very difficult and disturbed high school boys was a pretty young woman of twenty-three, who got more discipline and cooperation from her class than all the towering male teachers with half a century of experience behind them. This may not be true for another class and for another community, but there is plenty of evidence to suggest that the age of the adult is not a significant factor in determining the qualification of a worker with troubled youth.

### Race, Religion, and National Origin Are Not Significant

It is a sign of reversed prejudice to assume that a Negro young woman would prefer a Negro leader, a Jewish young man, an adult of his faith, or a Puerto Rican, somebody from his hometown. Except for the language barrier—which can be overcome—young people do not suddenly "feel at home" with somebody who bears superficial resemblance to themselves. It takes factors very different from skin color, accent, or a religious symbol worn prominently to make a troubled young person feel at home.

### The Achievements of the Adult Are Not Significant

To assign or promote a leader in terms of his own accomplishments—he was the leading contender in three states, he was the outstanding swimmer in the Olympics, or she has two doctoral degrees—may work with children up to a certain age (even there, this appeal is not very lasting or profound), but it is completely misplaced when it comes to working with young adults, who will feel rightly annoyed at this kind of salesmanship. Their reaction will be: "What am I supposed to do, ask for his autograph, or what?" They will form their own opinion about the adult who has come to work with them, and this opinion will be based solely on what happens between them as they meet and cautiously make contact.

## The Adult's Affect Is Highly Significant

This is not a matter of what you say or do, but of how you say it. Call it the basic attitude, the feeling tone, the instinctual reaction—it remains a basic requirement for people who want to work with young people. If we feel slightly repulsed by the long, unwashed hair, the dirty fingernails, and the way they slouch, we don't have to say a word—they will catch our repulsion. If we get the feeling that we are looking at a bunch of creeps, zombies from a distant planet, stop right there. They will not respond. If we feel like a G. I. who has just discovered a cave inhabited by Korean war orphans, to be adopted by CARE, if we feel pity at that much neglect, emotional or otherwise, we won't be accepted. If we think we know exactly what they need, if we come prepared with attitudes and opinions, books and records, and wide-eyed idealism, the young adults will not pay much attention to us.

Neither our training and our degrees, nor our theoretical understanding, nor our recommendations, will mean a thing when it comes to the affective reactions to young people. Long before we have spoken a single word, our feeling tone will be communicated. We don't hide it, and no cover-up will work for long. We may talk jive or act with studied detachment, we may say all the right things and look like a regular guy, but it won't work if we can't come with a genuine feeling of respect and equality, a sense of genuine interest, a sincere readiness to learn something about this particular young woman or group of fellows, if we don't have an inner ease and sense of being comfortable. Only we can know whether we "dig" young people.

If we have to ask how one gets this basic acceptance, forget it. It is like the rich man who was asked how much it costs to run a yacht and who rightly answered, "If you have to ask how much it costs, don't bother getting one." An adult has to be loaded with enough talent for work with young people not to have to ask how one gets compassion.

This is something we cannot learn in school or get from supervision. There are a great many things we have to learn, but acceptance of young people is not one of them. We have it or we don't. And if we don't have it, we shouldn't insist on working with young people. We may have the most unusual gift for small children, old people, young couples; we may do our best work with individuals or with small groups; we may have to find out, by trial and error, if we have not been exposed to many different kinds of human relations, but, as with talent in anything, each of us has an idea of what he can do best.

### The Acceptance of the Young Adult Apart From His Acts Is Highly Significant

Each of us as individuals knows whether he sees Susan Spencer as a "drug addict," or Mark Metcalf as a "make-out man," or Walt White as "a crazy kid." If we can't sense the complex, infinitely rich personality behind the presenting, disturbing symptoms or surface behavior, if we really, honestly think of a young person who has stolen a car as a "thief," an untrustworthy, basically dangerous crook who is halfway to Sing-Sing, we can't work with him. Nobody can tell us how to feel deep inside; if we can't, right away, sense the healthy potential of a Linda Lewis or a Gwen Grant, if we can't under-stand, stand under, get into their shoes, feel as they do, we would do better working with other people than youth.

If their language, their ways of dressing, their tastes in music or poetry, their choices of heroes and villains, their values—what they do and the way they do it—interests us, arouses our curiosity, makes us want to understand, we will be in a much better position than the many adults who get a headache from their records, feel sick, vaguely irritated, or mildly depressed when listening to them.

A group of parents of high school seniors, intelligent, middle-class people, said that they had heard the name of Bob Dylan, the folk singer, because "Our kids play his records all day long," but not one of them had ever sat down and really listened to what Dylan was saying. They all felt that the loud guitar, the noise, the hard-to-comprehend words were too much trouble. They were asked to listen to the "Ballad of the Thin Man," expressing loneliness and uncertainty and sung in a minor key with a bitter, melancholic guitar accompaniment. One could have chosen any of a number of such songs—to try to help the parents of these young people get a sense of what their kids are feeling, for the folk singers, who sell their records by the million, are popular because they represent a common feeling. The point is not whether this is poetry, or music, or art, or folk art. The only point of interest to us is that young people are listening to it and that the singer is communicating something to them.

This is part of accepting young people, quite aside from agreement or difference of opinion. That the parents had never really listened to Dylan is significant, because it shows a vaguely condescending attitude, which of course comes across in a thousand small ways.

If we are that far removed from young people, any young people, how could we possibly expect to have a really respectful acceptance of youth in trouble—people like Mark or Linda, who are so much more difficult to understand?

## To Particularize Behavior Is Important

Everybody has his own language; indeed, we can distinguish characters in a good play by reading only the dialogue, because each person's vocabulary is specific. In addition, we have cultural and local speech patterns, accents, idioms, peculiarities.

There are also characteristics of language in different phases of development, and young people have a language that best expresses their feelings and thoughts. When a young man says that he and his girl "split," one gets a graphic picture of sudden and sharp separation of two people who were too close and had merged. When Susan says, "I turned on," one gets the image of the sudden, mechanical movement in turning on a motor, a light, a record player. It represents the sudden flooding of a room with bright light, with sound by the least possible effort: the turning on of the switch. Susan inhales a few puffs of a marihuana cigarette and feels all "lit up."

If we'd ask Tom Tibbett how he was feeling, he would answer with a lecture on moods, differences between feeling and thinking, or the frustration in being unable to communicate.

Appearance, too, is specific. A young woman in college, who wore Levi's and suede boots, confessed one day that she would prefer skirts, but the crowd that she felt she needed for a sense of identity would turn their backs on her if she wore them. Until she no longer needed this identification and this image, she felt, she would go on wearing Levi's and suede boots. She was talking about the identity diffusion we discussed earlier.

There is no need to make any value judgment about the music or the books, the language or the clothes; the issue is to accept it and try to understand it by particularizing, instead of making generalizations.

There is group behavior—a platoon of Marines, a stage filled with choirboys, a meadow with Slovakian dancers—where the attempt is made to look and sound and act alike. This will do for the man who watches the parade, who listens to the concert, who comes to enjoy the folk festival. Those of us who want to work with troubled youth have not come to watch, to remain passive as an audience, to sit back and relax. Working with troubled youth is work.

### The Ability to Sustain Interest Is Necessary

This topic does not refer to what is commonly known as reliability, steadfastness, or any of the other sterling qualities usually attributed to the helping adult. Let us consider, rather, his ability really to remain interested in the problems of troubled youth, in the sense that he has a growing curiosity and a feeling of being challenged, as the first illusions of pat thinking and easy solutions make way for inevitable frustration, requiring more determined and concentrated effort. Working with troubled youth is like driving up a steep hill with the brakes on and no simple way to release the brake pedal.

Certainly, we have to be on time, ready for work, unhurried, and looking comfortable, but these things we can manage with discipline and goodwill. What is more important—and much more difficult—

is to be able to tolerate the continuing frustrations; the enormous amount of narcissistic self-involvement; the total absence of any genuine interest in us, except as somebody who can be used for the moment; the open or concealed hostility; the provocation and seduction; the speed and the sound of the work. To be able to remain genuinely interested in young people, with an awareness of where the healthy ego forces are, where the acting-out begins, where the superego interferes—all this, while we engage in an activity or a subject, requires a certain predisposition, a gift, or a readiness which we may or may not possess.

Another way of saying the same thing would be to emphasize that if we want to work with troubled youth, we had better prepare ourselves for a long pull, a slow and steady climb, a scaling of craggy mountains, not a pleasant stroll along a soft beach. This is important for our and their perspective and mutual expectations. Young people may lose patience with us and may want to give up; that's the privilege of their phase of growth. As long as we are prepared to stand by and go on working, whatever the difficulties, we may be able to help.

## A Conviction About the Healthy Ego-Core Is Fundamental

We could hardly be expected to work with troubled youth unless we had the basic conviction that there is, as the common saying goes, some good in everybody. Put in another way, it means that most human beings have the capacity for growth. It means that one or more functions of the ego are intact. It is a fact that even the most regressed catatonic, who lives in a state of perpetual sleep, can be reached. This means that even in the state closest to death, a remnant of the ego has been preserved. It is most difficult at times to remain aware of this fact, to locate the areas in the personality where the healthy forces are hidden, but anybody who cannot fathom the potential for health in troubled youth cannot help them.

Particularly with young people, who frequently seem to need to convince the world by their action and words, that they are "no good"; who seem to do all they can to prove to us that we are wasting our time and that they are lost and can never be changed—

particularly with these young people, we need to know, understand, sense, that there is something to build on.

What is the evidence of an ego-core? The very fact that the
young people are in front of us—in our office, our gym, our shop
or studio, our clubroom, or on our street corner—that they have
come . . . walked . . . moved . . . means that they have overcome
both the passive wish either to do nothing or to die and the primi-
tive hostility that wants to destroy whatever gets in the way of
immediate pleasure gratification. That they are there at all is evidence of some ego functioning. They may not be able to talk, and
they may not be ready to do anything right now, but they may want
us to do for them what nobody else had in the distant past.

The author has worked with a young man who came weekly,
without being able to say more than "Hi," and who started to cry
whenever feelings welled up in him. With him, the author had to do
most of the talking and to watch his eyes for response. The young
man communicated by mail when he was in college, writing long
and thoughtful letters. This happened ten years ago. He is today
teaching at a university and has a small family.

A sculptor friend has been working with troubled youth in an
empty store, teaching sculpture, clay modeling, and working with
stone. Among his group was one young woman who had been
making a living as a prostitute. The artist sensed immediately that
talking would not be the way to reach her. They talked only shop:
the legs and arms of the model, the making of an armature, the way
to wet down the clay, the roundness of the thighs and the major
lines of the face structure. In the two years that she worked in his
shop, he never asked her a single question or treated her differently
from any other student. He told her what she was doing well, and
he criticized her work when it was inept or superficial.

The group met at night in a blighted neighborhood, which to the
young woman had meant a profitable marketplace. In the beginning, she missed many a class; gradually, she came more regularly,
and one day, she asked the teacher about modeling jobs. He suggested that, instead, she continue her work as a sculptor, since she
was gifted, and make her living in some other way. When she asked,
he suggested a vocational guidance agency, which found her a receptionist job.

This was the beginning of her rehabilitation. To discover museums with the class, paintings, music, a world in which one could express many feelings in acceptable ways, was the bridge to a new and healthier self-image.

If we had asked the artist how he had happened to find a way to reach her, he would have looked at us without comprehension. "She was there, in the studio," he would have said, "so I gave her some clay. That was all."

He has not studied the theory of ego functions, nor would he particularly care to. This is not his field. But the fact is that he has a strong conviction about young people's creative abilities.

He did not start out with the intention of giving direction to this young woman's life. He has no illusions about rehabilitation, but he believes that somebody who shows enough interest to come to a dirty, cold, empty store and work with sticky, wet clay wants to create something. That's good enough for him.

Actually, it does not matter for our discussion whether he encourages a talent, or steers—as he has done—some young men into making dies for industry, when he found there was no gift for sculpture. What matters is that he finds the ego, the available resource in the young person, and on it builds a constructive self-image. Like the X ray that customs inspectors use to discover hidden diamonds, this man has an eye for the most valuable, though hidden parts of young people.

In a school for emotionally disturbed adolescents, the staff would, at times, spend half a day in a clinic session, trying to understand a particularly difficult youngster who was not responding to therapy, work programs, or education. Very often their last resort was Jack, the man who ran the farm attached to the school, who in the past had been able to reach youngsters with whom nobody in the clinic could make any progress. The author tried to learn from him by watching him work. Jack's language was coarse, his manners harsh, his movements and commands brisk, yet some of the most disturbed young people came back to their cottages in the evening after some time with Jack smiling, talking to other young people, and even willing to see their therapist. How did Jack do it? One got an idea by sitting next to him at lunch in the central dining room. The way his eyes laughed, the way he shrugged his

shoulders when told about the boys' delinquencies, his feeling about
the young people, which was based on a conviction, based purely
on intuition, that there is a sound core in people, if only one can
get to it.

If we have this gift, this talent—which is as valuable as the talent
for writing novels, composing music, or directing a play—we can
then use our skills, our training, our learned, acquired know-how
in helping young people.

There exists in the population a great, untapped resource of men
and women who have the right feeling for young people, but who
have not had any professional training. They may have wanted to
get more education, but were not able to do it for reasons of
finance, age, and family responsibilities. They are sometimes afraid
to offer their services, because they have been over-impressed with
the importance of training, just as some of the trained people have
underestimated the art of communication, which cannot be taught.

Of course we need both, intuition and knowledge, but where an
adult is sought out by young people—which often is the best proof
of his innate ability to understand—he need not shrink back and
look desperately for the man with a degree. When young people
seek him out, he has something to offer that is extremely valuable.
It is not the activity they engage in that matters, but the fact that
somebody cares. The sensitive adult who has the confidence of a
troubled youth, will also be in a very good position to recognize
when more help is needed than he can offer.

However, his recognition of the need for professional help as
well as the young adults' readiness for it, may not be sufficient because there may be no professional workers in his hometown. This,
in spite of the fact that we have in this country a small host of
professionally trained workers, ranging from counselors to psychoanalysts, with services ranging from an occasional contact to four-
times-weekly sessions, with fees ranging from fifty cents to fifty
dollars.

Walt White had a wide choice in New York City: clinical
psychologists or psychoanalysts, guidance counselors or family caseworkers. Gwen Grant had no choice at all. Since she did not want
to talk to the old priest in the small town near her farm community, there was nobody competent to work with her. In the

middle-sized town in which Linda Lewis lived with her mother, there is one family agency, with one young woman who is competent with troubled youth. There also is a vocational guidance agency, set up for testing and helping with vocational choices. Linda was not able to work with a woman, and there was no man available trained to work with her. She did not need vocational guidance services, but intensive therapy to resolve her sexual conflicts.

Why the distribution of professional workers for troubled young adults is so uneven is a complicated question, having to do with community planning, social and economic issues, and a number of other sociological causes that we cannot discuss in the framework of this book.

The lack of available resources, the high cost of treatment, the uneven distribution of professional people are, however, additional factors that complicate the helping process. Even if a Gwen Grant has recognized that she has problems, after she has finally gotten ready to do something about it and has come to terms with the idea of forming a new relationship with a professional, she has the problem of finding somebody within commuting distance, and within her family's budget.

Because of this situation, it is understandable that where these shortages exist, the professionals, in their desire to relieve misery, tend to try to be all things to all men.

## Education, Counseling, and Therapy

The bulk of full-time professional work with troubled youth is carried by the educators, the counselors, and the therapists. Although these three large professional areas overlap to a small degree, people will get the maximum of help if the educator teaches, the counselor suggests, and the therapist practices therapy. There are some schools of thought that advocate a minimizing of professional distinctions. They take this position for a very understandable reason, stated above: Since many communities only have one teacher or one clergyman, it is most "realistic" if these overburdened, hardworking professionals do whatever they can to help

—a little education, a little counseling, and some therapy, if absolutely nothing else is available.

From all the evidence in very different communities and with a variety of disturbed youth, it seems highly unlikely that this approach works, in practice. The three different professions have different aims, objects, and methods of work. Because of this, their professional training has had different theoretical orientations. Unless a teacher has, in addition, studied counseling, unless a counselor has, in addition to his profession, had special training and supervision in therapy, they can be more helpful to young people if they practice what they know well.

Not only does each of the professions have its own orientation and well-thought-out curriculum, but young adults very often react with justified doubt and suspicion when a specialist in one field subtly crosses over into a neighboring profession. The guidance counselor who offers tutoring, the therapist who selects "the best" college, the teacher who probes into fears of learning, are typical illustrations of professionals leaving the area of their competence, and with it, weakening their effectiveness in helping troubled youth.

We do not have to become rigid when we emphasize the boundaries of the three major helping professions. They do have much in common: they all aim at change, they all use language as their tool, and they are all based on the behavioral sciences. Yet, the very strength of each profession rests—as in the ego of the individual—on a clear recognition of boundaries and limitations. In order to sharpen the awareness of these boundaries and limitations, an attempt is made here to delineate the three major helping professions by distinguishing each by its aim (*what*), its object (*where*), and its process or method (*how*).

## Education

AIM:     Without attempting to define the learning process, we can say, for the purpose of this clarification, that the aim of education is to impart knowledge and skills. Implied in this aim is the giving of information and facts to the learner. A related function is to exercise mental functions, the ability to think in orderly, rational ways, to learn, through constant practice, to use facts to draw rational conclusions. In the acquisition of skills, there is the implied aim of enabling the student to use skills and facts constructively, for his personal use or the benefit of others. We are aiming at a better comprehension of man and nature, we are aiming at a deeper understanding of the laws of nature and society, we are aiming at the accumulation of meaningful knowledge, the richer and deeper understanding of man and his world.

OBJECT: In pursuing this aim, we are concentrating all our efforts on the conscious ego of the student, although we are aware of the fact that unconscious factors and instinctual drives play a prominent part in the psycho-biological process of learning. We are also working with the superego of the student, the part that from earliest childhood represented the realistic demands of the outside world. We are teaching values, what is right and wrong, strengthening the ego in its battle against passive and regressive wishes.

PROCESS: In the context of this discussion, the primary method used in education is the group process, the interaction between peer group formations and the leader of the group, the educator. The awareness of the individual needs of each student, as distinguished from the needs of the teacher—the recognition of the subgroup formation; the effect of group contagion; the management of the highly complex group dynamics—all this constitutes the basic method of the teacher in the classroom. By creating the appropriate group climate, the teacher provides the individual student, who is also a part of the group, with the knowledge that he aims to impart.

## In Brief:

In *education,* the aim is the imparting of knowledge, which means the teacher directs his efforts to the conscious ego and the superego of the student, via the direction of the group process.

## Counseling

AIM: Without attempting to distinguish between the various schools and aspects of counseling—vocational, family, marital, pastoral—we can say in the context of this discussion that the aim in counseling is to enable the client to cope better with currently active conflicts, centered around specific issues. With this, the counselor aims at his client's ability to use his resources to the best possible advantage and to recognize, as well as he is currently able to, his limitations and his assets. Implied in this goal is the effort to enable the client to adjust to his environment, or to change environmental conditions according to his recognized self-interest.

OBJECT: Contrary to education, counseling directs itself primarily to the most intact aspects of the client's ego and deals with the superego only when it is too rigid or punitive and interferes with the smooth functioning of the ego. Unlike the educator, the counselor does not form an alliance with the client's superego. When he tells his client, directly or indirectly, what he "should" do, the counselor has subtly crossed over into the field of education. He cannot be judgmental—as the teacher, he cannot be critical—as the teacher has to be, he can make no demands and give no assignments. While he, like the teacher and the therapist, should be well aware of the unconscious interferences, the resurgence of infantile drives and early conflicts, he cannot direct his efforts at the early instinctual derivatives, or the preconscious manifestations. His particular training and his defined relationship to his client limit him to deal in his sessions always with these aspects of the ego that are accessible to him. His role, because of the object available to him, has some built-in frustrations: he always knows much more than he can use; indeed, much of his knowledge of ego psychology and the unconscious is useful precisely as a guideline for the available ego boundaries.

PROCESS: Unlike the method in education, the counseling process usually takes place in a face-to-face relationship, in which the counselor attempts to enable his client to verbalize his problems. This, by itself, brings relief because the ego can face verbalized ideas better than unclear, vague emotions. The presence of a counselor—a clergyman or a physician, for example—who can listen with interest and empathy to a client's or patient's worries brings substantial relief to people who have nobody else to talk to, or who have been misunderstood or scolded for their difficulties.

The counselor may make new connections for his client between hitherto unconnected aspects of his personality, tracing behavior patterns, which can help the client to function more effectively. He may confront his client with realistic limitations, based on objective test findings or material from interviews. The skill in using confrontation requires not only tact and common sense, but also knowledge of the many—and often hidden—ways in which feelings or fantasies are expressed.

Another aspect of the counselor's method is the manipulation of the environment, or the attempt to enable the client to make environmental changes which are in his interest. The family counselor—often a trained social caseworker—may work not only with his client but, at times, with other members of his family in order to enable members of a family to make a better adjustment to each other.

If, for example, a counselor in a guidance office learns that a young man's learning difficulties are considerably aggravated by an anxious parent, he may make suggestions about the course of study and, the student willing, arrange for some sessions with the parent and another worker in order to help the mother to help her son. This would be a different parent interview than the classroom teacher can conduct.

### In Brief:

In *counseling* the aim is to enable the client to cope better with currently active conflicts, centered around specific issues. The object of the counselor is the client's ego, which requires a thorough knowledge of the field of ego psychology. He works in a face-to-face relationship through the method of objectification, practical adaptation within recognized limits, and manipulation of the environment.

## Therapy

AIM:          Therapy, indicated when counseling cannot do the job,
aims at resolving basic, early conflicts in order to enable the ego
to cope adequately with current conflicts. This means that there
had to have been early damage to the ego, sufficient to prevent it
from functioning in all areas. It may function in some areas of
behavior, but not in others. In his last writing, Freud enumerated
eight specific functions of the ego, in regard to external and
internal events:[1]

1. becoming aware of stimuli from without
2. storing up experiences of them (in the memory)
3. dealing with moderate stimuli (through adaptation)
4. learning to bring about appropriate modifications in the external world to its own advantage (through activity)
5. gaining control over the demands of the instincts
6. deciding whether they shall be allowed to obtain satisfaction
7. postponing that satisfaction to times and circumstances favorable in the external world
8. suppressing their excitation completely.

When the ego fails to function in most of these areas, when the
individual, as a result, experiences more pain than pleasure, then
therapy rather than counseling may well be necessary.

OBJECTS:          Unlike education, which is directed to the most rational part of the ego and the often overused superego, unlike
counseling, which works primarily with the intact part of the ego,
therapy has to focus on all parts of the personality. The therapist,
in order to accomplish his aim, has to work with the instinctual
drives and their derivatives in consciousness, the expressions of
the early wishes in dreams, and the ways in which they are distorted by inner censorship. He has to work with the superego and
the ways in which it weakens or strengthens the ego, wherever
it needs reduction or modification. He works with the defenses
of instinctual wishes and the healthy defenses of the ego. He
works with the conscious ego and the unconscious and forgotten
parts of the early ego. He works with the present and the past,
the role of the environment now and long ago, fantasies and

daydreams, realistic and unrealistic thinking—in brief, with the total self.

PROCESS: In order to get a thorough picture of the many different parts of the personality, the therapist often will try to teach his patient to free-associate; that is to say anything that goes through the surface of the mind, without any censorship or premeditation. Only by eliminating intellectual prejudgment can the patient expose the total complexity of his mental apparatus. Unlike the educator, who asks the student to think before he speaks and to talk sense, unlike the counselor, who tries to get his client to deal practically with reality as it is, the therapist wants his patients not to censor any thought or feeling, whether it seems to make sense at the moment or not, whether it sounds reasonable or irrational, in order to discover the processes that interfered with the healthy functioning of the ego. This manner of talking in therapy is difficult for people to learn, and may be resisted in many different ways. The therapist's job is to help his patient to overcome his resistances.

Where the teacher speaks and lectures, where the counselor interprets tests and behavior, the therapist listens more than he speaks, in order to learn something about the complex mental mechanisms, the nature of his patient's defenses, the manner in which the patient uses the therapist as part of the therapeutic process, which is a re-experiencing of earlier feelings to make them accessible to rational observation.

## In Brief:

In *therapy* the aim is to resolve the basic early conflicts in order to enable the ego to cope adequately with current conflicts. This aim requires focusing on all parts of the total personality—the derivatives of instincts; the ego, conscious and unconscious; the strength and weakness of the superego—on the present and the past. In order to achieve this aim, the therapist frequently uses the method of free association, and through meaningful interpretations, enables the patient to experience once more in the present, what caused the impediments originally in the past.

This brief, general description of therapy does not tell us anything about the many different forms of psychotherapy, the many
schools of analytic thought, and the variations in both individual
and group therapy. Some of what constitutes the most intensive
form of psychotherapy has been described in a previous publica-
tion, where the process of treatment is discussed as well as the
training of the practitioner.[2]

When professional help is needed—provided that there are
resources in the community—the parent or the leader of young
people is likely to get the most objective advice about choice of
counselor or therapist through the local family casework agency.
The trained social worker has the skill to screen the problems
presented and make an intelligent referral to a psychotherapist,
a guidance counselor or any number of community services.
Many family caseworkers have themselves been analyzed; in
some of the oldest and best-established agencies psychoanalysis
is practically a prerequisite for employment. The workers in
these agencies have a real concept of what is involved in various
forms of therapy or counseling, are trained to think diagnos-
tically, and are familiar with psychological testing services, as
well as with psychoanalytic and other therapies available in the
community.

*In Brief:*

The primary prerequisite for working with troubled youth is the
absence of fear, which exists among many groups, both professionals and lay people. The primary qualifications are neither the
adult helpers' age or sex, their race or religion, nor their accomplishments, but their affect, their ability to accept young adults aside
from their actions, their capacity to particularize behavior, to
sustain interest over a long and difficult period of time and, most
significantly, to recognize the healthy core of the ego in young
people.

Where the ego has been so fractured that treatment is indicated,
specialized help is called for but may not be available in a given
community.

In spite of our desire to make up for the shortage of trained workers and for the uneven distribution of them the country over by trying more than we are capable of, we can be of the most help to troubled youth if the teacher teaches, the counselor counsels, and the therapist does therapy. Toward this end, the boundaries of education, counseling, and therapy have been outlined.

# 13

# Once More: Six Young People

This book started with brief sketches of six young people. Throughout, they have been referred to, aspects of their character and behavior have been discussed, and their parents briefly met. Some characteristics of young adults have been discussed, as have the difficulties in being really helpful to them. Now we may want to take another look at the six young people, in the light of our added understanding. We may also be interested in how they have fared.

When we last read about them, two of the young people had been married (Tom Tibbett and Gwen Grant), two had gone into institutions (Walt White and Susan Spencer), one had planned to enlist (Mark Metcalf), and one was living by herself, continuing her acting career (Linda Lewis).

How have their families helped them or failed to reach them? Has there been a clergyman or a counselor who has made a difference in their lives? Have they been fortunate enough to find somebody who has the gift of compassion? Have some of them received any benefit from psychotherapy?

## Tom Tibbett

Actually, it was the young nursery-school teacher, whom Tom had married, who kept after him to do something about his indifference. Very soon after they had begun their married life, she became concerned about Tom. Not only his gaining weight and his constant complaining about his market research job, but also his unwillingness or inability to get close to her or their little boy, his lack of interest in other people and the world outside, became more and more alarming. His new manner of not talking much, his lack of genuine interest in anything, the way he came home tired and bored every day, the hungry way in which he ate and then went to sleep— all of it was not the Tom she had known in college. Obviously, he was not happy, but if she asked him, he denied it and assured her that everything was fine. He did what his employer or his wife asked him.

Once a week he took wife and child to visit his family, ate dinner, made small talk, and after going through the motions of putting the baby to bed, watched some program on television for a little while and went to sleep. He was not eager to make love to his wife; he did not enjoy playing with the child. He got no kick out of a small promotion on the job, nor their first summer vacation.

After his wife kept after him for nearly a year, Tom had to agree that perhaps he should talk to somebody he felt confidence in. To her surprise, Tom did not choose the minister who had counseled against marriage, but drove the fifty miles to his alma mater and looked up Professor Weston, his old adviser.

He had *recognized* some of his problems and was getting *ready* to do something about them. Although he had no clear idea of what was needed, he did experience that feeling of clouds lifting from the mind as he drove up the winding dirt road that led to the campus.

Professor Weston greeted Tom warmly, but after making his visitor comfortable, settled down to the role of the attentive listener. He had sensed very quickly, from looking closely at Tom, that what the young man needed at this moment was to be allowed to talk freely, without interruptions, without probing questions. He was a sensitive counselor who, partly from past knowledge, and partly from his intuitive grasp, made it possible for Tom to verbalize many of the feelings that became more conscious in this office, as he took the difficult step of giving words to emotions. Theoretically, Tom was moving from a preconscious sensation to fuller, conscious awareness, a process which by itself brings relief and furthers the process of getting ready to form a therapeutic relationship. Tom was not concerned with judging his own expressions or with deciding whether or not what he felt was practical or very rational. When he said that he hated his job, when he talked about feelings of indifference about his wife, of irritation about his child, Tom was not worrying about his counselor's reactions. Professor Weston had provided a climate in which Tom could talk without fear of being judged.

The counselor, with his focus on the conscious ego, noticed that one word stood out in everything Tom said, a word that was repeated time and time again. The word was "should" and represented Tom's rigid superego, the original interference in his self-image dilemma, his identity struggle.

At the appropriate moment, when he sensed that Tom was ready to consider this conflict, the counselor pointed out that Tom seemed to be preoccupied with what he felt he "should" do. Tom was startled at first, but understood what Professor Weston meant when he repeated some of Tom's statements. For the first time, as far as he knew, Tom recognized the existence of a harsh inner policeman, who seemed to have gotten the upper hand in his character development. If he had always done what he felt like doing, he said, he might have done nothing at all.

Like some other overconscientious young people he had known, Professor Weston understood that Tom too had coped with his early instinctual wishes and strong impulses by clamping down on them with a punitive, overdeveloped superego, without allowing the ego to have a chance to intervene and mediate, according to reasonable and feasible standards. In other words, Tom's ego had not developed to its fullest capacity, and needed to be rebuilt, freed from the clutches of the superego, and given the chance to guide the self toward its healthy capabilities. It was also clear to the counselor that the tasks of rebuilding the ego and of finding a better way of coping with early conflicts would have to be performed by the man trained for this job: a therapist.

By using the material Tom had given him, the counselor was able to show the troubled young man that he was continuously struggling with an inner conflict which had been expressed in the form of withdrawal from his family and a lack of interest in the world at large.

While Tom was not ready to see the inner conflicts, he could not deny his tendency to isolate himself and to live, as he himself put it, "on two cylinders only." He said that the talk with Professor

Weston had helped a great deal, and expressed the natural desire to see his old adviser again. At this point, the counselor faced the most difficult moment in his interview: the time to declare the limitations of his ability to help, without hurting Tom's feelings—and to arrange for a transfer to a new relationship with another person, trained for the job.

Tom reluctantly considered this idea, but withdrew again when the counselor mentioned the form of help needed: psychotherapy. Like countless others before and after him, Tom suffered from the ago-old prejudice against psychiatry, psychoanalysis, clinical psychology—any contact that, in his eyes, would label him as "crazy." All his intellectual knowledge, the textbooks on mental hygiene he had read and discussed in psychology classes, and his forum discussions on schools of psychoanalysis to the contrary, when it came to his own treatment, Tom acted like a man who had no idea what psychological illness means. He began to think in black-and-white terms of "sane" and "insane," instead of the realistic continuum between illness and health, which is a matter of degree, not of kind.

He heard his counselor tell him that illness and health are not absolutes, that we are all more or less healthy or disturbed, and that his conflicts had tipped the balance toward pathology where treatment was indicated. Professor Weston suggested a psychotherapist near Tom's hometown and expressed the hope that the young man would consider working out his conflicts with this qualified specialist.

While Tom had been able to recognize some of his problems, and had been ready enough to see the counselor, he was not quite ready to form a new relationship with the therapist. Even after he had reconsidered his prejudice against treatment, he hesitated, finding ever new excuses—lack of money, lack of time, many rationalizations, all of which he discussed with his wife. In spite of her encouragement, Tom was not ready to take the last step in the helping process, until a few additional symptoms tipped the balance. Occasional signs of near impotence, forgetting two important appointments, and one near accident, which he himself recognized could have been avoided by more care on his part, forced him to reconsider Professor Weston's suggestion, and got him ready to call the therapist.

After the initial uneasiness in the strange office, Tom said that he had been sent by his former adviser, Professor Weston, but was at a loss as to where to begin. The therapist told him, with a friendly smile, that he had already begun by talking about Professor Weston. Perhaps he could continue to talk more about his old adviser. As Tom recalled his experiences with his adviser, it occurred to him that, early in his college career, there had been a rather difficult meeting concerning the editorial of the school paper. When the therapist wondered whether the professor had objected to Tom's editorial, it occurred to the patient that what had made the meeting difficult had been Professor Weston's concern about Tom's falling marks, due to over-involvement in community activities. Talking about it now, it occurred to Tom that his eagerness to get lost in social action had far preceded his parents' interference. He told the therapist that until this moment, he had been convinced that it had been his father's interference that had steered him on the wrong course.

"Professor Weston had no objection to my editorial," he said, reflectively. "He wanted me to bring up my marks and not get lost in social action. I don't know why I didn't listen to him. Until now, I was sure that the meeting had been about the editorial and academic freedom."

The therapist suggested that there were many reasons for this slight memory distortion, which would become clearer as they would retrace their steps together and come to understand both what had made Tom get so involved and what had prevented him from considering his adviser's suggestions.

The words, "retracing steps," made Tom think of other episodes in high school, where he had been torn in similar ways.

"I've always tried to do justice to everybody," he said, "and still stay on top. I guess it can't be done."

"It sounds," the therapist commented, "as though you must have been fighting with yourself for a long time—almost as if you had two opposing value systems inside of yourself. Could they represent your parents' opposing values?"

Tom nodded slowly, puzzled for a moment at the therapist's correct guess, but then comprehending that his conflicts might well be obvious to an objective outsider.

If one could pinpoint the moment when somebody is ready to begin a therapeutic *relationship,* it was this first hunch of the therapist that convinced Tom of the wisdom of working out his conflicts with somebody who had the compassionate neutrality and the skill to help him.

After another interview, the therapist suggested that Tom plan a full psychoanalysis, since he was relatively healthy enough to permit the uncovering of defenses that occurs in this form of therapy. Although Tom had some difficulties in accepting a four-times-weekly therapy, with the concomitant cost, he worked out a graduated plan in which hours would be slowly increased, while the fee was lowered to enable him to use this preferred form of treatment for Tom's form of neurosis.

As is usual in analysis, some of the latest surface symptoms—which had triggered his beginning treatment—were modified first and disappeared in a relatively short time: the mild impotence, the forgetting of important appointments, the hazardous driving, and similar self-destructive tendencies. Although both Tom and his wife were happy about this change, he fully recognized that the resolution of the early conflicts, the modification of a rigid superego, and the full functioning of a potentially healthy ego, would take much longer than the modification of the surface symptoms. In spite of the ever-present resistances to change, Tom understood that since the analytic process represents a re-experiencing of early conflicts in which the analyst is used in various roles, the uncovering and rebuilding of the ego would take several hundred hours.

There seems to be little doubt in his analyst's mind that Tom will continue to associate and analyze his resistances and that he will, in time, give his ego the chance to develop to full capacity, so that one can expect that Tom is on his way to getting ready to use his energies, his excellent potential, to build a constructive and satisfying life for himself and his family.

### Linda Lewis

Linda, the young woman nicknamed in high school "the woman beautiful," who went through one unhappy lesbian relationship and a very brief, unsuccessful marriage episode, has basically not changed, and in all likelihood is not going to change very much. If we saw her at night, sitting in her favorite bistro in Greenwich Village, sipping espresso from a straw, her long legs in tight Levi's stretched out in front of the little marble table, we might believe what her friends would tell us: that "Linda has a ball."

Unlike Tom, she has never for a moment recognized that she has problems, that she is in trouble and needs help to straighten out her life. When, on some rare occasion, some older girls, or the owner of the bistro talk to her and encourage her to "see somebody," Linda reverts back to her high school level and tells these friends that "headshrinkers are stupid" and that she is through with "mother figures and all kinds of do-gooders." She announces, in no uncertain terms, that she needs no help.

After her brief marriage broke up, her mother physically took her to a small private clinic of which she had heard from a neighbor. Linda went, unwillingly, slumped on the chair in the psychologist's office, and said nothing. The therapist encouraged her to tell him what was on her mind, but Linda let him know that there wasn't a "damn thing" on her mind. She smoked one cigarette after another, looked out the window, and yawned with boredom. When the man asked her whether she wanted to make another appointment, she laughed in his face and asked him whether he were kidding.

She never returned to this or any other clinic, and told anybody who wanted to know about her that she was "through" with all that. She talks to people on the job, in her acting classes, in the house where she occupies one small room, or in the bistro where she spends her free evenings.

Not that she talks about her problems. She does not see herself as the cause of any of her difficulties. She complains about her mother, the way she has been "exploited," about the lascivious theatrical "sharks" who promise her parts and want only to go to bed with her. She talks about the unfair casting system, the unfair conditions on the job, the unfair landlord who does nothing about cockroaches or heat, the "fairies" wandering around her street all night, the crowded subways, the high cost of living—the unfair society in which she has to live.

Linda lives a marginal life, both emotionally and economically.

She has many casual acquaintances, no real, close friends. She has brief sexual affairs, mostly with older men, but occasionally again with women. She manages to hold on to her job as a receptionist, she succeeds in getting an occasional walk-on acting part in a small theater, she manages to pay her rent, she manages to survive by eating stand-up lunches and occasional, quickly made hot meals. She moved into a neighborhood where she knew she would find many other lonely young people like herself, so that she is seldom alone, and can avoid facing herself and her inner conflicts. When she, on some long, empty weekends, feels too blue or lonely, Linda gets comfort from having a few drinks in the local bar at the corner, where she is sure to find some people she knows or meet some new people who are bound to pay attention to her, because she has remained a strikingly attractive young woman. Her dark bangs nearly covering her large, expressive eyes, her straight black hair framing her small, pale face—she still frowns on lipstick—Linda manages a mysterious smile, suggesting deep secrets and talent and wonderful things to come.

It is most important to her to keep "cool" at all times, not to get excited or upset at anything, no matter what. The *self-image,* which she is maintaining, is that of the alienated, detached, isolated, "modern" young woman. She can be seen at a "happening" in town, at the opening of an "art show" in which magnetized television pictures are distorted on the screen, or an "avant-garde" music festival in which the audience leaves the hall to return with garbage cans, coffee cups, or hub caps—any objects they can find—as part of a "composition" by one of the young people who call Linda by her first name. She may be on the stage or in the audience of a "dance recital" in which a bizarre figure stands stock still, center stage, for ten minutes while weird electronic "music" whirs through the darkened hall.

Since she has never solved her *identity dilemma,* Linda merges symbiotically with any person or object or movement that is "new," because this suggests to her originality and uniqueness—since it had not been done before. The confusion between content and form does not occur to her, even though she would be perfectly capable intellectually to comprehend the basic issues involved.

Since she has not been able to cope with the *time-continuity* problem characteristic of this age, Linda exists in a time vacuum, avoiding the realistic fact that she is getting older, that in fact, she will soon be too old for the parts she wants to play in the theater, or the fact that she has no theater credits to her name, which, for an actress in her early twenties, is a problem, particularly since she claims to have been studying for seven years. As far as time is concerned, Linda chooses to believe that her break may happen tomorrow, and since in this field, occasional breaks of this kind do happen, she feels that she is completely realistic in her assumptions.

In many ways, Linda has not faced the *end of role playing,* but has remained emotionally on the level of adolescence. She attempts to build her life on the few segments of her ego that are intact, while acting out as many of the early fantasies as she can.

She is doing it by making the role playing as real as possible. She will say on her job that she is not a receptionist "really," but an actress, who is making a living. In the acting studio, she announces to visitors that she is not an actress "really," but a "student of the drama." In her rooming house, she is not a tenant "really," but an "actress at liberty." In the bistro, she is not a beatnik "really," but a working girl who wants to relax. Nothing is for real; everything is a role.

Can anybody help Linda? Her mother, who tried—even though in a way that was not constructive, has given up after Linda told her in no uncertain terms that she wanted to be left alone and had no desire to see her mother ever again. The innumerable attempts to come with home-cooked meals, to invite her out for a good time, to send her a check to help with expenses, were all rebuffed. Linda wants no part of her mother, and this is one thing she really means and does not merely play as a role.

The friendly people around her who have suggested help, or offered a helping hand, have been rejected. Linda wants no help from anybody.

What will happen to her?

The police captain of her precinct, who knows Linda from two holdups at night, says he expects to find her battered or dead one night in a dark alley. He is convinced that she did not have to get into the situation where she was held up and nearly raped late at night. "If she would take better care of herself . . . ." says the captain. He means, in terms of ego psychology, if her self-preservation would function adequately, she would protect herself against danger from the outside. He says with wry humor that he almost wishes she would get herself into real trouble, so that he could send her to Bellevue, because, as far as he is concerned, "This is a sick little girl."

The captain is right. Linda is a sick little girl, but she has not been able to master the *Three R's Of Helping,* and until she does, nobody can help her. This is a heartbreaking realization, but a necessary one.

But perhaps the captain is unduly pessimistic. Perhaps Linda will survive and succeed in her field. We can certainly hope so, even though we have little basis for optimism, except for the knowledge that Linda is not the only young woman who is disturbed. She is not nearly as unusual as she likes to think she is. There are a great many disturbed people in our society who manage to survive and who never get any help. It is not for us—who would like to help— to say how people should live their lives. Still, we cannot help wishing that there would have been something one could have done for Linda Lewis.

## Walt White

Unlike Linda, who plays with reality, Walt's disturbances had reached the point where he was no longer able to distinguish sharply between reality and fantasy. The difference is one of degree—as is all health and illness—but it is a significant one. If Linda says that she is between engagements, she knows that she is trying to cover up for her lack of success by distortion of reality. When Walt says that he is engaged to his former piano teacher, Miss Daniels, or when he hears people talking, although there is nobody in the store, he is not role playing; he believes sincerely in what he says. His fantasy has become his reality. The core of the ego is damaged and all functions are impaired. When an individual, like Walt, has reached this state, he may be certified for commitment to a mental institution by two qualified psychiatrists, according to the legal definition of sanity and insanity. While this definition has been under scrutiny for a very long time, it still operates and explains why Walt, at the request of his very distressed parents, is being treated in a state hospital. This is one exception to the laws of the helping process, when somebody is being treated without having asked for it. Many people ask for treatment in a hospital and commit themselves voluntarily, but the majority of cases in state hospitals are so-called certified cases—non-voluntary commitments.

There are, of course, many hospitals operated, not by a state, but by private organizations and supported by public contributions. Such hospitals accept only voluntary commitments because they are convinced that the chances for a cure are best when the laws of the helping process are functioning, that is, when somebody has recognized the need for this kind of intensive therapy, is ready to spend some time in the hospital, and is able to work with one of the therapists in the hospital. Frequently, these private hospitals expect the patient or his family to contribute financially toward the therapy, while state hospitals usually do not charge for their services.

The White family had no choice but to use the state hospital, where Walt underwent the standard medical, psychological, and psychiatric examinations, after which he was placed in the adolescent ward. The thorough physical examination revealed no pathology; even his headaches and eye strain appeared to be functional, rather than organic. Neither the electroencephalogram nor the head X rays showed any abnormalities; the ophthalmologist found his eyes in good condition, his glasses appropriate for his visual deficiency. All the major organs were in excellent shape; the blood count was normal—in a word, physically, Walt was in fine shape.

It was very different when the report from the clinical psychologist came in. After he had administered the standard projective tests (the Rorschach Test, the Thematic Apperception Test) in addition to the Wechsler Intelligence Scale, and the Drawing of a Human Figure, the psychologist scored each test according to Walt's individual response, interpreted them according to the scientifically validated and accepted concepts, and totaled all responses before submitting the summary of his findings.

It read in part as follows:

. . . Walt's reactions to all the psychological tests are of such an order as to suggest that he is suffering from schizophrenia. Significant for such a diagnosis is his variable approach to reality, his thinking disorders, the fluctuations he manifests in meeting the demands of reality; the fluidity and vagueness of his ego boundaries, and his marked preoccupation with problems involving "wholeness" and relatedness. He vacillates between experiencing himself as so tied to the irreconcilable aspects of himself that he can not get away from these (a feeling that is well symbolized by such Rorschach interpretations as "two Siamese twins joined by their backs, by their backbones, by their spines. They look like they're trying to pull away from each other"). Contrarywise, as someone "cut in half," to use another of his test productions. . . .

His difficulties are of an all pervasive order, having impact on his emotional, interpersonal, sexual and intellectual functioning. However, despite the seriousness of his disturbances he is not without resources, nor is he emotionally inaccessible. Thus, although he is likely to be quite withdrawn and unpredictable, it seems possible that he can be helped to develop a more positive integrated concept of himself . . .

The social worker who had interviewed Walt's parents emphasized in her report Mr. White's passive, carefully controlled hostility, and a tendency toward isolation and withdrawal, while it appeared to her that Mrs. White represented the powerful, benign, but controlling mother, who seemed to have been the dominant force in Walt's attempt to find an identity.

After the psychiatrist had had a long interview with Walt and basically agreed with the psychologist's diagnosis of schizophrenia, the team met to map out a treatment plan for him.

While there was a preference for individual therapy, the final compromise was group therapy, to expose Walt to a controlled situation of peers, in which his relationship distortions could be worked out, but primarily because this hospital, as most hospitals, did not have nearly enough experienced therapists to cover the needs of the large patient population. The psychiatrist assigned a gifted young psychiatrist resident to be responsible for Walt's case and to see him as frequently as possible—with the many demands of intake, clinic, and inpatient service that are made on residents everywhere.

The clinic team remained mindful of Walt's creative expressions, which in the past had been a source of satisfaction to him, and arranged for him to work twice a week in the occupational play-room where the teacher in charge would be apprised of Walt's ability in drawing and painting. The social worker attempted to get regular piano practice time for him, but this suggestion was not accepted because of schedule difficulties as well as the psychologist's suggestion that the more isolated activities would tend to draw the patient further away from the peers on the ward and would most likely provoke the hostilities of the other boys that Walt had expe-rienced in the past. Instead, the clinic team agreed to give him the opportunity to play the piano for as many social functions as pos-sible—during ward parties or for recreational activities.

Since Walt had appeared very withdrawn in intake, the psychia-trist prescribed five milligrams of dexomill, twice daily, a mild stimulant which he believed would be sufficient at this time. He left open the possibility of stronger drugs, but suggested that the case be reevaluated in two weeks, after Walt had had a chance to adjust to the new environment.

Since Walt had been neither homicidal nor suicidal, he was placed in the open pavilion, where the doors were not locked nor the windows barred, and where the attractive grounds were used by the patients.

When his mother came for her first visit, Walt told her that he liked it "here." He seemed to make good use of the art workshop, took to the young psychiatrist, and found the group therapy "inter-esting" because it had been his first experience in which he was protected from ridicule and verbal abuse by peers. He had discov-ered that he could talk, since he was sure that the doctor "is on my side." By the third week, he attended his first party with girls, when the male and female adolescent wards had been allowed to plan a joint Halloween party. While Walt was encouraged to make up any costume he liked, the art teacher saw to it that the young people did not act out the most bizarre or frightening ideas. There were sufficient adults—group workers and volunteers—around to super-vise the party carefully in such a way that nobody got hurt or upset.

Since Walt took to the institution, he did not find it too difficult to talk to his doctor or the social worker, who soon learned to translate his particular language and distorted meaning, without criticizing him.

The young patient never had had so many people interested in him, trying to understand him with his peculiarities, and providing the protection which his disturbed ego had not been able to develop. Except for occasional unpleasant scenes with more disturbed ward patients, and the dull food, Walt liked his new environment. When he told his parents during his first home visit, six months after his commitment, that he was looking forward to going back, he was quite sincere.

As for prognosis, nobody on the clinic team is willing to make an outright prediction. Everybody is encouraged about Walt's progress, but nobody is able to know how this temporary adjustment to a specialized environment will work out once he is released. Nevertheless, the art teacher has begun to encourage Walt to join the letter shop, and hopes to interest him in the print shop later on. Walt finds lettering easy, and told his social worker that he is looking forward to learning the printing trade, so that he can have a "good job" once he is out of the hospital.

His parents dream of the day when Walt can come home, learn to make friends with young men and women, and hopefully, meet a girl he will marry. When they asked the social worker about Walt's chances for a normal life, she did not assure the family, but told them that it is difficult to know in this kind of illness. She based this on the clinic's evaluation that Walt is doing as well as can be expected with this much pathology, but that the prognosis must remain guarded.

## Gwen Grant

It would never have occurred to Gwen to get help for herself. She had always been the "I-don't-count" girl, and continued this attitude into her marriage to the widower and his child. When her anxieties over her role as a good mother led to serious overindulgence of the little girl, the first difficulties appeared—curiously, not between Gwen and the child, but between the child and the father. He noticed a lack of respect on the part of the little girl, a tendency to whine and insist on getting what she wanted, some difficulties in reading, and bed-wetting, which had stopped several years before. In spite of all his assurances, Gwen was convinced that the child's behavior was a result of her handling. It was all her fault. She tried harder to please and indulge the child, with the result that the symptoms increased.

When the difficulties began to affect the relationship between Gwen and her husband, they agreed to seek help, and saw the clergyman whom the husband had consulted before, after his first wife's death. It took the clergyman only a few sessions to decide that Gwen was, without knowing it, unable to set firm limits for the little girl. In talking to Gwen alone, the counselor understood that Gwen was simply not able to say No, to give the child responsibilities, to help her effectively. Unless the young mother would get some help to become more objective about the child, things were likely to get worse. At the same time, the counseling clergyman understood that Gwen was in no way ready to accept help for herself. She would, however, do anything in the world, to help the little girl. With this clear insight in mind, the clergyman suggested the local family agency as a source of help for the child's difficulties. He explained to Gwen the ways the people worked in the family agency, assured her that they had helped other children before, and, with Gwen's permission, made the first appointment for the child—and her mother.

It is important to recognize that the clergyman's sensitive referral paved the way for all the subsequent benign developments in Gwen's and her family's life. If he had insisted on emphasizing Gwen's problems, she would have withdrawn defensively and never gone near any helping source. By utilizing her devotion to the little child, the counselor made it possible for Gwen to become ready to face her own fears and anxieties—though much later on.

Gwen went with the child to the family agency, stayed with her and the caseworker in the playroom where the first work took place, and after a few weeks came willingly alone: to report on the child's history and development.

Not until Gwen suggested that many of the child's troubles were her (Gwen's) fault did the caseworker shift the focus of interest from the child to the mother. The skilled worker simply asked the client to tell her more of what she had meant by the self-accusation, and with this question, gave Gwen the opportunity to talk about herself, while the worker listened attentively. Noting the enormous amount of guilt, the hidden anxieties, the deep feelings of insecurity and inadequacy, the worker decided to move very slowly and allow Gwen to establish a trusting relationship in which she could feel free to say eventually things that she had never said to anybody: the early feelings of hostility, the competitive feelings with her older sisters, the attachment to her brother, the deep dislike of her mother. None of these feelings were expressed until almost a year after Gwen had first come to the agency—as the child's chauffeur.

Quite naturally, while the child saw her worker, Gwen became accustomed to talking to her own caseworker, and came to look forward to talking. While she had had no intentions in the beginning to talk about herself, she found herself revealing details of her own handling of the child and experiencing some relief from having a professional, interested person listening to her. Very gradually, Gwen felt freer to tell what she called "little secrets" about herself, and was both astonished and relieved that the worker's attitude did not change, no matter what was said. Very slowly, very cautiously, Gwen tested out her new confidante. One week, she mentioned, seemingly in passing, that she had felt critical about her husband's handling of money in a restaurant: he should have left more of a tip, as seen from a former waitress's point of view. The caseworker made no comment, but nodded understanding, and later on, suggested that Gwen might be critical of her husband on other occasions as well. Gwen still could not believe it, but it appeared that no matter what "awful" feelings she expressed—feelings she had harbored and hidden for years—the worker never got angry or impatient like her mother. It seemed almost incredible, but here you could say anything at all, without being criticized or chided, accused or punished.

In the meantime, the child had been helped by her worker, formed her own relationship, and one day, announced that she could take the bus to the worker all by herself—leaving Gwen free to recognize that both she and the child had independent helping relationships.

When Gwen was making her appointments in the morning—

separate from the child—she fully recognized that she was in treatment herself. While she usually started each session by talking about the child, the worker gradually freed her of this obligation and helped her to recognize that Mother herself was a person in her own rights: a young woman with her own troubles, many of which had started long ago.

Gradually, Gwen began to talk about her own past, her need to be a "good girl," to gather the firewood for the Girl Scout cookouts, about the many baby-sitting jobs, the seeming necessity to be "nice" to everybody out of fear of being disliked.

She discovered, in the relationship to her caseworker, that she did not have to be "nice" to be accepted and respected. She could get angry without withdrawing into silence, and she could say the kind of things she had never said out loud. Whether her anger came from the worker's being late for an appointment, or from the dislike of an interpretation, Gwen discovered that it helped to talk. Nobody disliked her for it, nobody was about to send her away.

Her greatest frustration and anger occurred when she could not get the worker to answer her questions about handling the child. The caseworker was not taking the role of the *educator,* but remained with the focus of her job, the weakened and poorly developed ego of her client. When Gwen, for example, would ask what she should do when the child refused to put on her boots in the snow, the worker did not offer advice, but suggested that Gwen felt very frustrated and angry at the child for not obeying. Gwen had to admit that one of the reasons why she had not taken a firmer stand with the child was her fear of being hated by the little girl. What she could not yet face were her mixed feelings of love and hate about the child, and the fact that this ambivalence prevented her from being able to take a realistic, firm stand. As the parallels to her own childhood were drawn, Gwen could admit tinges of jealousy of the child, who had it so much easier than she had had it at that age.

There were also current feelings of jealousy when she hesitantly talked about her husband's being so much more concerned about the child than about his wife. Gwen faced, for the first time, the fact that her way of coping with these feelings—trying harder to please everybody—did not work. This was another new discovery which, like the others, gave her an entirely new concept of herself and her behavior with her family. She had to admit that until now, she had never much thought of herself, but had always tried to do "the right thing," which to the caseworker meant, living by the commands of the superego, a way of life which is not realistic and has to lead to anxiety and guilt.

When Gwen talked about helping the child with homework, the caseworker sensed her client's preoccupation with the child's doing extremely well in school. Once this was explored, it appeared that Gwen was still suffering from the fact that she had not finished high school or gone on to college, as had her older sisters.

Long-buried ambitions and aspirations came to the surface, as the casework process progressed—a desire for a child of her own, the dream to become a teacher, the hope for a wider cultural horizon, a less sleepy town, an interest in books and music; a whole world seemed to open up, as Gwen started to face herself.

In the meantime, her ego had grown sufficiently to handle the relationship with the little girl without quite as much guilt as in the past. While it was still hard for Gwen to say No firmly, or to tell the child to put on her boots, she was able to do it with more and more conviction, particularly because Ellen responded to the new quality in her mother's voice. At the same time, the child had been enabled to express many of her conflicting feelings about her mother to her worker, which in turn, helped the mother-child relationship.

The little girl did not want to return to her worker after the summer, but Gwen asked for a second weekly appointment, because it seemed to her that she was just beginning to discover what she was all about. As she put it, when she talked to her husband, it was like being born all over again.

The young woman who, most of her life, felt that she did not count is beginning to discover that she is a unique human being with distinct characteristics. She is discovering that she is valuable and that she can love without pain.

## Mark Metcalf

When the Air Force rejected him, Mark was very upset. Being turned down by a branch of the military service had more of an effect on him than most other experiences during the preceding few years. It certainly meant more to him than having had to appear in court after his involvement with the beach house destruction; it meant much more than having been asked to leave camp in the middle of the season, after he had been found in a compromising position with one of the girl campers; it was much more meaningful than his few talks with the psychiatrist or the near tragedy in which two girls became pregnant. All of this he had been able to shrug off, to take in his stride and joke about. Not the rejection from the Air Force.

His father, as in the past, tried to console him by assuring him that the tests he had passed with low marks were unnecessarily technical; by making light of a spinal curvature that had never bothered him; and by joking about the army psychiatrist who, in his routine examination, had gone extensively into Mark's "delinquency record." Mr. Metcalf was convinced that these men "raised hell" in camp in their own way, but got high and mighty when it came to misdemeanors of wild young kids, who, like Mark, never had meant any harm.

But no matter what his father told him, Mark remained disturbed. For the first time, he doubted his father's integrity, and wondered whether what his father told him was really very good for him. He appreciated his mother's dry comment after he announced that he could not enlist, "What did you expect?"

Not only was the rejection a painful experience, but it also forced Mark to cope more realistically with his future. His original plan to "get away from it all," by joining the Armed Forces, had not worked out, and he had to continue with college and his job in the store. But while these activities were tolerable, he was most downhearted that he had to see his probation officer, according to the court order, following the hearing.

He would appear in Mr. Kay's office in the municipal building, looking sullen and thoroughly annoyed, barely willing to talk. Mr. Kay, the probation officer, a young man with some training in counseling and casework, was used to young people coming to him in this state of mind. He had thoroughly studied Mark's background, his school record, and his encounter with the camp director, and had had a conference with the therapist who had seen Mark a few times. Unlike some of his colleagues who wanted nothing more than to be promoted to administrative positions and climb the ranks of the civil service, Mr. Kay liked his job and liked young people. He was an easygoing, thoroughly friendly man who did not have a trace of hostility in him, and was able to have a friendly smile even when young people like Mark did everything they could to be disagreeable and provocative.

Before Mark had a chance to express his resentment about having to come, Mr. Kay told him that he knew that Mark felt like a criminal and resented having to report to a man whom he considered a plainclothes cop. Mark gave the man a long and searching look, but did no more than shrug, as if to say, "Big deal."

The probation officer suggested that as long as they would have to meet every two weeks for the next six months, they might as well talk together.

Mark told him that if he had not been interested in talking to the "shrink" (short for "headshrinker"), he saw no reason why a probation officer should expect him to talk. Mr. Kay thought that what Mark said was quite true, but that it might just be more interesting to talk a little, rather than just sit here.

Mark considered this and, in a burst of anger, told Mr. Kay that if the Air Force had accepted him, he would not have had to go through this whole business. Since Mark seemed motivated to talk about his rejection by the Air Force, Mr. Kay asked him about the details of the interviews and tests, a topic which still had much meaning to Mark. To Mark's surprise, the probation officer's response was completely different from that of his family and friends. Mr. Kay neither consoled him nor defended the Air Force. He agreed with Mark that such an experience can be very upsetting, but suggested that like other upsetting experiences, or even tragedies, one can get over the feeling in time.

Although Mark protested that this was easy for a man of Mr. Kay's age to say, he nevertheless felt some relief from the friendly objective response which contained neither reproach nor consolation.

When it came close to leaving, Mark wanted to know when they were going to talk about the "court business," and was again surprised when Mr. Kay assured him that while the court had made him report here, there was no rule about the content of their discussions. What is discussed here "is up to us." The use of the word "us" suggested a common interest between himself and Mark, who left, shaking hands and feeling much less angry than he had when he came in.

The good feeling lasted from Mr. Kay's office to the clothing store, where Mark was due for work half an hour later. He immediately switched to his role of the agreeable, polite young businessman when he waited on his first customer, while that evening he yawned through a long lecture in class prior to a date with a new girl he had met the day before. He did not give another thought to Mr. Kay until he had to report again, two weeks later, when he came in with the same anger as the previous time and left with the same friendly feeling as before.

In other words, there was no carry-over from one interview to the next, regardless of Mr. Kay's warm interest and skillful handling of the young man. Mark, like some very young children, was interested as long as the experience lasted, and lost interest as soon as it was over. Nothing that was discussed made any impression on him or remained longer than the interview itself. This was true for the experience with Mr. Kay and with the therapist he had seen a few times; it was true for his classes and for his personal relationships. He hardly remembered the girls with whom he had slept, and he gave them no more thought than he gave to any other experience.

When Mr. Kay, one day, brought up the destruction of the beach house, which had led to the court hearing and the probation, Mark looked solemn and chagrined. He thought that he had made a mistake in getting drunk and losing control, and did not think the fun had been worth the trouble he got himself into. He was not interested in talking about possible causes for the behavior or about the danger of a repetition. He doubted that he would go as far the next time "round," but thought he would stop short. He assured Mr. Kay that he was watching his step and saving his money, because he wanted to buy himself a sports car and go skiing, come next winter, while in the summer he definitely planned to learn surfboarding. One day, when he could afford it, he would like to learn flying a plane and to own a little Cub.

He finished his friendly talks with Mr. Kay, and took the full-time job in the clothing store when school got too difficult in the second year. He likes the job and likes living at home, where he continues to be helpful and pleasant. While he is getting too old for the title "Make-out Man," his relationships to girls are the same as they ever were, except that he now inquires whether the girl is taking "The Pill."

It is unlikely that Mark will change very much in any area of his character, because he does not experience enough—pain *or* pleasure—to be motivated for the major effort required for inner changes. He is a little more careful in his social behavior, and has no intentions of establishing a home of his own, or getting married. He cannot see the point of having to worry about somebody who lives with you.

From all indications, Mark is going to live with his problems: his shallow affect and his character disorders, his inability to sustain interest, and his unresolved homosexual problems.

It would appear that he has learned to avoid causing trouble to others, and to plan his life in such a way that he can manage it. Without recognizing it intellectually, Mark seems to have learned to live within the limitations of his personality. If we would ask him if he is happy or at least content with his way of life, Mark would answer in the affirmative.

## Susan Spencer

Cliché thinking, labeling, and scapegoating are only a few of the obstacles to understanding of young people, but they are standard fare among some young people themselves, particularly those who have gotten into enough trouble to have been institutionalized, like Susan Spencer at the Briarcliff School. Before the bus from the Shelter had even arrived at the administration building in the Westchester Hills, the mysterious grapevine which operates in all institutions and small living units had pronounced Susie the "drug addict," "the easy lay," and "the best-looking smart cookie."

Boys on lawn detail, girls in the trade building, stopped working and came to look. In spite of the supervisors' objections, the young men leaned on their shovels and rakes, the young women left their sewing machines and beauty parlor operator machines, and converged on the bus: Susie was famous before she ever set foot on the neatly gardened grounds of Briarcliff.

While the boys were fighting among themselves to decide who was going to "get" her, the girls united very quickly into a hostile reception committee, bent on "breaking her in right."

After a day of getting acquainted with teachers and clinic personnel, people of her own age, and the routine of school, laundry, central dining room, and recreation, Susie was accompanied to the cottage where she was to live with fifteen other girls, about half a mile from the main campus. While the cottage mother, a firm and friendly older woman, welcomed the newcomer and got her established in her small room, Susie got the first feeling of open hostility from the few girls who were assigned that day to clean thoroughly the living room downstairs. When the cottage mother introduced Susie, the girls did not even look up from the floor, but continued to scrub and wax, as though Susie had never entered the room.

That night, a contingent of the girls provoked a fight with the newcomer in which all the repressed sadistic trends were acted out in the most brutal way, in near silence, which was arranged by clamping pillows over Susie's face while the ringleader forced a broomstick into her rectum, leaving Susie in agonizing pain until morning, when she slipped out of the cottage, ran away from the landscaped grounds, and took to the highway before dawn, the first of many "AWOL" expeditions.

The State Police, notified by the Administration, picked her up before she had reached the city and brought her back to Briarcliff, where she had her first session with her social worker. Tight-lipped and acid in her withheld rage, Susie made it clear that she was not going to break down and cry, nor was she going to "rat" on the girls in her cottage with whom she would have to live, for at least a year of her "prison term." The role she decided to play was clear: cooperate on the surface, shut up, and get through this as painlessly as possible. No, she was not going to break any rules, she was not going to touch "pot" if it were handed to her, and the "punks" in the boys' school had another guess coming if they had any ideas about *her*. "Just tell me what to do and I'll do it, but leave me alone and don't give me that sympathy bit."

After four months of weekly and twice-weekly therapeutic sessions with both the psychiatric social worker and the consulting psychiatrist, the clinic admitted that they were getting no place with this case. Susie stayed precisely within the role she had carved for herself, and was not to be persuaded to go beyond it. The psychiatrist, a very experienced clinician, kept the sessions at first on a friendly, social basis, allowing Susie to talk about Briarcliff, the rehabilitation systems, Youth and Freedom of Speech, Cultural and Political Activities, and Susie went along pleasantly, until the doctor shifted to a question about Susie herself, when she blocked and announced that she was not going to talk about that at all.

Asked about her determination not to work on her problems, Susie declared that she was managing her problems in the institution, and invited the psychiatrist to check her record: she was attending classes, doing her homework, carrying out her chores in the cottage, not getting into fights, not smoking pot or fooling around with boys. When the doctor asked, smilingly, whether she considered herself a model patient, Susie nodded and agreed. As long as she could control herself in this way, she could see no reason to "dig" into the causes for her troubles. And when the doctor suggested that working on the deeper causes might stir up unpleasant memories and forgotten experiences which seemed to be too painful, Susie agreed. She had had her share of misery and she was not about to cause herself more trouble. She was no "masochist."

When the psychiatrist inquired whether she would be willing to talk about her future, instead of the past, Susie expressed mild interest. She would discuss practical things, but nothing "personal."

This seemed to be a fruitful approach at first, but after several sessions, it turned out to be another hollow victory for the clinician. It became quite clear to the clinic team that while they had a very interesting folder in their drawer, full of tests and many pages of interview notes, data from the Shelter, the public school, and the court, none of this knowledge was being put to any use whatsoever. Susie was marking time, behaving impeccably in the institution, providing no ground for discharging her, or declaring her incorrigible. In fact, Susie was not in therapy, but merely going through motions.

In one of the evaluation conferences in which, besides the clinic team, the teachers and visiting art specialists participated, the psychiatrist announced the failure of his team by declaring that nobody was reaching the girl. There seemed to be agreement from the school teachers and the cottage mother, the shop teachers and the supervisor who had seen Susie work in the dining room and the office.

The one exception was Miss Langer, the woman in charge of the drama workshop. To everybody's surprise, Miss Langer reported that Susie was participating actively in the writing of a new play, that she had personally stayed on after class, missing recreation and free period, to rewrite a scene. In the specialist's opinion, Susie was gifted as a writer and perhaps in acting as well.

Briarcliff had long recognized the values of the arts in conjunction with therapy, because for some people, the nonverbal or disguised expressions of complex feelings have made communication possible. It was in Miss Langer's workshop where a depressed boy, who could not speak a sentence without stammering and stopping on every syllable, was able to read a part he had helped to write, without any speech impediment whatsoever. Miss Langer, a specialist, lived on the grounds and pursued her workshop with a missionary zeal. Occasionally she spent her free time or a whole Sunday with a few young people who had become involved in the creative process, which she believed was sometimes the most powerful method of sublimation.

The young people who had chosen her workshop from the available art workshops—music, painting, sculpture, dance—spent several long and relaxed sessions discussing ideas for a play that would interest everybody enough to work on writing it themselves. Miss Langer believed that if somebody chose her workshop and participated in the sessions, he would quite naturally express feelings, since they were talking about nothing else but characters and their emotions.

With a thorough grounding in the theater, Miss Langer resisted the temptation of facile substitution of the young peoples' problems by the characters they created. Believing firmly that everybody basically writes about himself, the instructor discussed the characters, not the writers, and treated her students the way she had any other group of students of playwriting and acting. Within this professional atmosphere, Susie felt free to talk and contribute, since she never felt "like a patient etherized upon a table," as she described her clinical interviews to Miss Langer in an informal coffee hour after a drama workshop meeting.

Again, as in every attempt to help, one cannot know what prompted Miss Langer not to refer to Susie's knowledge of the Eliot poem, but to accept it as something the young woman must have loved. Call it intuition, tact, wisdom—it was the right thing for Susie, who felt safe with this woman, while she had been unable to allow the other workers in Briarcliff to make close contact with her.

Although the new insights about Susie were shared with the caseworker, who observed a lessening of hostility in the girl's responses, the major source of help to Susie was the drama teacher. The feedback from the creative to the therapeutic process was of great value to the clinic team, but nobody doubted that without Miss Langer, Susie would have passed through the Briarcliff year unchanged, and with no contact with her inner conflicts.

Apparently, Susie was gifted in writing, according to Miss Langer and the English teacher, who helped her to get a scholarship in a small college. Since Briarcliff had insisted on a trade besides, Susie had perfected her typing and was now able to hold a part-time secretarial job in the college town, supplementing her scholarship income.

The great thrill was the acceptance of one of her short stories by a small literary magazine, which paid her twenty-five dollars, her first earning as a writer. That she sent this check to Miss Langer as a contribution to the drama workshop—notorious for its budget struggles—suggested to Miss Langer and Susie's former therapists that the girl was changing. Nobody knew much about her relationships to young women and men of her own age because Susie did not speak of them in her letters to Miss Langer, whom she considers her "Mother Superior," as she put it. She does keep in touch with this teacher, and occasionally includes in her letters torn pages from her writing notebook. They are never dated, but she suggests whether the enclosed is current or past writing. One of the enclosures read as follows:

"Yes I will die and not be worth the effort to reincarnate.
They don't like me.
I don't like me
I hate my character
I want out
I want out
I want out!
Please help me, for thine is the power—
Help her to help herself—no good, too hard
Either love or forget her—
I want out
Yes, I will live in hell
And never be allowed the luxury of death
No way to go on
No where to run
*no where* to hide
I want out NOW.

Now it is settled into a dull pain.
I hate it.
Why?
What makes this girl different from all others?
Everything.
Forever
I will wait for him. He is not here. He won't come.
I will turn in; the outside is more than I can handle—
The inside is safe and warm
The inside is sleep and pot and music
And most of all, no people.
No people, no people.
Help me
I am a little, lost sheep
No, I am just lost—
Lost sheep are by definition found.
No one knows I'm gone
No one would care . . ."

This page of Susie's letter had on the margin the notation, "written some time ago," a fact to which Miss Langer referred when she

answered. She surmised that if Susie were to write a poem today it would not be as sad as this one. From all one knows, things look brighter for Susie these days, particularly since she seems to be enjoying school, writing, and talking about a boy, whose name has been mentioned more and more consistently over a period of a year.

## *In Brief:*

The questions posed at the beginning of the chapter were answered with brief follow-up reports of the six young people. Once they had been in trouble, their families were no longer able to help them. All of the six young people had had experiences with sources of help outside the family: Tom with psychoanalysis, Linda with clinical psychology, Walt with group therapy, Gwen with family casework, Mark with counseling, Susie with therapy in a controlled environment, where the drama teacher was of crucial significance.

Four of the young people made good use of the available resources: Tom, Walt, Gwen, and Susie. Two were not able to benefit from the help offered: Linda and Mark.

# Notes

## Part II—Some Causes
### Chapter 8—The Young Adult (I)

1. Rudolph M. Wittenberg, *Adolescence and Discipline* (New York: Association Press, 1959), pp. 40–60.
2. Jean Piaget, *Play, Dreams and Imitations in Childhood,* trans. C. Gattegno and F. M. Hodgson (New York: W. W. Norton & Co., 1952).
3. Anna Freud, *The Ego and the Mechanisms of Defence,* trans. Cecil Baines (New York: International Universities Press, 1946), pp. 149–66.
4. Rene Spitz and W. Cobliner, *The First Year of Life* (New York: International Universities Press, 1965), pp. 178 f.
5. Sigmund Freud, *An Outline of Psychoanalysis,* trans. James Strachey (New York: W. W. Norton & Co., 1949), pp. 13–19.
6. Erik Erikson, *Identity and the Life Cycle* (New York: International Universities Press, 1959), p. 150.
7. Edward Glover, "Metapsychology or Metaphysics," *The Psychoanalytic Quarterly,* XXXV, No. 2 (1966), 185.

### Chapter 9—The Young Adult (II)

1. Eric Goldman, *The Crucial Decade* (Vintage Books paperback ed.; New York: Random House; orig. publ. by Alfred A. Knopf, Inc., 1956), p. v.
2. *Ibid.,* p. 123.
3. Dean McIntosh, as quoted in *The New York Times,* May 10, 1951.

4. Goldman, *op. cit.,* p. 265.

5. *Ibid.,* p. 301.

6. *Ibid.,* p. 305.

7. *Life,* March, 1957.

8. Goldman, *op. cit.,* p. 316.

9. "Kids and Money," *Look,* November 2, 1965.

Part III—Some Solutions

Chapter 12—Working With Troubled Youth

1. Sigmund Freud, *An Outline of Psychoanalysis,* trans. James Strachey (New York: W. W. Norton & Co., 1949), p. 15.

2. Rudolph Wittenberg, *Common Sense About Psychoanalysis* (New York: Doubleday & Co., 1962), chapters 1 and 7.